Keeper

Keeper

A Life Amongst Fishes and Those Who Catch Them

By Martin Donovan

DEPARTURE

Keeper

A Life Amongst Fishes and Those Who Catch Them

Departure Publishing LLC
PO Box 160818
Austin, TX 78716
(512) 347-8336
www.departurepublishing.com

First printing: May 2011

ISBN 10: 098338570X
ISBN 13: 9780983385707

Edited by Dave Lawton, Cazenovia, NY
Book design by Peter Morris, Smashing Designs, La Jolla, CA
Original artwork by Bob Whitc, Marine on St. Croix, MN
Printed by Bang Printing, Brainerd, MN

To my Dad, Pat Donovan, who taught me how to behave, respect, listen, learn, and countless other lessons – apart from how to play football or cast a fly rod!
In loving memory of my Grandparents, and my darling Mum, Ruth Donovan. A loyal friend to everyone she met, and an adoring "Granny" to Hannah, Gareth, Paul, Jodie, Sean, Rebecca, Andrew, Reece, Alice, Michael, Ben, Zoe and Neve.

"Happiness, health and good luck always."
- Ruth Donovan

Acknowledgements

There are some special people whom I would like to thank for all of their help and support with this book, and my career as a riverkeeper.

Firstly and especially, a heartfelt thanks to my gorgeous wife Jo, and our children Jodie, Alice, and Michael. A prouder husband and dad you will not find.

For my brother Christopher, sisters Helen and Clare, and to Jonser. To Barry and Joyce, Alan, Jackie, Max, and Harvey.

To all of my friends on football pitches, golf courses, cricket fields, and riverbanks; and in curry houses, public houses, and fishing huts.

For Vic Foot, Ron Holloway, Jon Hall, Paul Moncaster, Fred Kemp, Pat Moyle, and others who have taught me the ways of a riverkeeper.

For Neil Freeman who has restored my faith in owners of fishing beats, and to my fishing mates John Hackney, Paul Ness, and Graham Backhurst who have always given me wonderful advice, friendship (and finance).

And finally, to my publisher Tosh Brown: I always suspected it would take an American. Thanks, mate.

Contents

A Foreigner's Guide to the Queen's English

Arse
Several meanings, all of which can be used in numerous forms of both compliment (she's got a nice arse) and insult (he's a real horse's arse).

Anorak
A foul weather jacket often worn by boring and meticulous people, such as train spotters and birdwatchers.

Bivvie
Short for bivouac. A temporary camp erected in the open air, which will inevitably fall down in the middle of the night.

Boiler
A pint of mixed beer (half brown ale and half mild bitter) usually fancied by underage lads and old men; a common denominator being lack of taste. Sixteen-year-olds have no idea what good beer tastes like, and old men don't really care anymore.

Boilie
Foul smelling bait balls most often used by carp fishermen. Used in such quantity that lake levels have been known to rise.

Bollocks
British slang for testicles. Can also be used to describe an exaggerated truth (that's a load of bollocks), something exceptionally great (that Spey rod is the dog's bollocks), or a form of exclamation (oh bollocks, not the bloody hedge!)

Brolly

Short for umbrella. Used by coarse fishermen who have forgotten their bivvie.

Bugger

A mild expletive never to be uttered in prison or at choir practice.

Cravat

A brightly coloured necktie worn as a sign of poshness or haughty upbringing.

Cricket

A British derivative of baseball, or vice versa, depending on whom you ask. Many cricket enthusiasts have one thing in common: no grasp or understanding of the actual rules.

Fag

In England: a cigarette. In America: a homosexual male. We'll stop there.

Football

A game played worldwide that does not involve helmets or cheerleaders. The English invented it and they're now not very good at it.

Ghillie

An Irish dancing shoe, or a dreak and soggy Scottish fishing guide whose glass is always half empty.

Git

By definition: an annoying or despicable person. More often used these days as a light-hearted insult aimed at English men by their wives (you miserable old git).

Kelt
A salmon or seatrout that has completed its spawn
(see "knackered").

Knackered
Completely exhausted (see "kelt").

Legging it
Running for your life, often from Irish poachers.

Marmite
A black and gooey yeast extract that can be spread on a sandwich
or used to season meat. Marmite on toast is as English as not speaking to each other in an elevator. Most people either hate Marmite,
or really hate it. Some claim that Marmite is the reason why beer
was invented.

Piss
To urinate, or an English/Australian slang for alcohol, especially
American beer.

Pissed
In Britain: drunk, or getting drunk. In America: angry, or getting
angry, often at those who are drunk.

Priest
Something (often incorporating deer antler) or someone (usually
dressed in a long purple cloak) to administer the last rites to both
human and fish. The fish gets a bash on the head by the deer antler
and the human is forgiven for previous sins by the man in the
purple cloak.

Quid
One pound British sterling, or one hundred pence.

Slag off

To tell the harsh truth about someone; always more effective when done behind their back.

Spate

A flooded river, typically found in Scotland during the prime salmon runs, or whenever the author is there.

Springer

An English spaniel that was bred to run full-pelt for at least twenty-three hours a day. Or, an increasingly rare, highly-prized, spring-run Atlantic salmon.

Tannoy

A device that typically turns the announcement, "The train from Liverpool will shortly arrive on platform four," into a scratchy and unintelligible noise.

Toff

Someone who often claims to have met the Queen Mother, rides a horse side-saddle, and is prone to getting a red nose when drunk. Fishing toffs always carry an empty wicker basket and ask for change from a fiver when tipping.

Tosspot

Same meaning as "wanker," but more appropriate when spoken among mixed company.

Wanker

An English/Australian term of guarded endearment. Sometimes referred to in Hampshire as "Bashing ones Bishop." Muttered on the chalkstreams in equal measure by both keeper and fisherman, often at each other (see tosspot).

Callings

y Dad always said that he found me as a newborn under some purple comfrey about a hundred yards from the River Test. It wasn't until about twelve years later that I realised he was pulling my leg and that I'd actually screamed my first lungful of air down the corridors of Lyndhurst hospital in Hampshire, England.

Even though my Dad's version sounded better, I still spent most of my childhood playing in or around that famous chalkstream. Our house backed directly onto the Lower Test Nature Reserve and we had direct, unimpeded access to the delights of the riverbanks that we treated as our own playground.

At age fifteen I escaped from Testwood School and the last sentence on my final comprehensive school report reads as follows: "Martin is a lovely boy and a credit to the school, however, he is far too much of a gentleman to get on in life."

I didn't give it much thought at the time but I can still remember my Dad being completely lost for words. All that he had ever taught me about the way to behave, the way to conduct myself, and the priorities of school life were dismissed in that one line written by a bored teacher filling out her umpteenth report, that day.

It was 1979 and Pink Floyd had just released a now legendary song containing a line relevant to almost every schoolboy in the land.

"All and all you're just a, 'nother brick in the wall."

My Mum and Dad thought attainment was nice, but as far as they were concerned it was secondary to effort and behaviour. I can remember my Dad taking me to play football at the local park and then spending ninety minutes watching the wrong game on the adjoining pitch. After getting changed, I pointed out to him that he'd been watching the wrong game, to which he replied, "Never mind my son, did you shake the referee's hand?"

That was my Dad.

I hated Testwood School and vividly remember that the best thing about it was the day I left. The next best thing was the day before I left. The third, and probably most important best thing about Testwood School was that out of many of the ancient sash windows you could look high across fields and meadows, through oaks and ashes and great copper beeches, and if the light was right, you could see the sparkling waters of the River Test.

I endured hours and hours of geography lessons, learning of English Kings and Queens, of religious education, and of the delights of mathematical theories—all whilst sitting, head in hands, and staring out towards those meadows and the world in which I so needed to be. This education lark wasn't all it was cracked up to be, I wanted to be on the river. Like most teenagers, my life seemed at the time to be going wrong—and what with punk rock, pubes, and rebellion, being attracted to a river wasn't the sort of thing that you could share with your spotty mates.

"That new Motörhead album is well cool, and have you ever wondered why ranunculus never grows in deep water?"

I was living in eternal conflict, and it didn't help that my dentist had a mouthful of black teeth, my barber was as bald as a badger's arse, and my doctor always had a bad cough. I was, I think, having a mid-life crisis at least thirty years too soon.

Some people think that their destiny is pre-planned and that their lives are already mapped out before them; just sit back and enjoy the ride. Others think long and hard about every decision, believing that the smallest mistake could ruin their whole life's plan.

Me? My way of life was inadvertently influenced by a tired school teacher, a teacher who hardly knew me, and who certainly didn't understand me, a teacher whose only worthwhile observation of me after years of honest endeavour (and lots of staring out the window) was that I was just too nice. What my teacher failed to realise was that while I may have run from school on that memorable last day, I was only trying to catch up with my desire to learn, which had died about two years previous.

This book started when someone asked me how I became a riverkeeper. Since that's not a question that I could possibly answer in a few sentences, I decided to start jotting things down. During that process, it became clear that my love of the chalkstreams and the fish were subconsciously developed at an early age.

What follows is a collection of stories and events from my childhood days of exploring and fishing on the River Test, a few odd jobs that influenced my perspective on life, and twenty-five wonderful years of cutting weeds, chasing poachers, tending fish, and guiding anglers.

Paper Boys And Kelts

ishing was a way of life for me and my neighbourhood mates. We spent most of our time trying to catch grey mullet and the occasional slob trout (a want-to-be seatrout that goes no further than Southampton water). Everything caught was returned to the river, apart from the odd mullet taken home to prove to Mum that we could actually catch something. Mum felt obliged to cook the mullet, but as I remember she never actually ate much, herself. If you've ever eaten mullet you'll probably know why.

Most of our fishing was done on the tidal section of the Test estuary with a float and bread as the bait. Although we did catch the occasional fish, it was more through luck than judgement. Many of our fishing trips were cut short for a swim, or a bit of den building, or other important business. We found that inflated tractor inner tubes made the ultimate boats, and each day usually regressed from serious fishing to just messing about on the water, a most noble of pastimes which I still practice to this day.

This all changed in the early 70's when we heard someone saying that seabass find worms irresistible. None of us had ever caught one and we suspected that they would almost certainly taste better than our usual offering to Mum, whom, we thoughtfully decided, needed a mullet break. Bent on catching Mum a proper fish, we unearthed some worms and actually succeeded in catching a few seabass. She was delighted.

Quite often, however, some great swirling monster that was certainly not a seabass would inhale our worms, break our tackle, and compel a long walk back to the house for another float. After many long walks and much lost tackle, my Woolworth's reel had very little line left on it. Fortunately, our next-door neighbour, a proper sea fisherman, gave me one of his old reels ready-loaded with plenty of line of about fifty-pound breaking strain. This was duly taped to my rod and I returned to the river with renewed enthusiasm.

The next swirling monster that ate my worm once again took off into the distance, and I stood waiting for the usual sound of a .22 rifle firing as the line snapped, while contemplating another tackle journey to the house. Surely I would lose this fish, and I was thinking that I just might give up fishing for the day and blow up another inner tube, when I suddenly realized that the monster and I were, in fact, still connected.

The as-yet-unseen fish had turned and was now heading at incredible speed straight back toward my mates, and me. It was towing about a hundred yards of line when it went past and its bow wave was similar to that of the Isle of Wight ferry. The great loop of slack line cutting through the water was struggling to keep up, and I literally hung on to the rod like a nervous water skier completely nonplussed as to what my role was in this unfolding drama.

After about ten minutes of the fish doing non-stop lengths of the section of river in front of us, it finally began to slow and I carefully…and very quietly…began to breathe again. By this time, my mates had all been attracted and stood behind me like great fishing sages coming out with indispensable advice learnt over many years on the river. The main consensus seemed to involve my reeling in the considerable length of line, probably about three hundred yards, to see if the monster was still on. The general agreement amongst the sages was that the fish was probably the mother of all seabass, although dolphin and indeed basking shark were mentioned.

After another ten minutes of reeling in slack line, we had almost given up on seeing anything and I for one was not particularly worried, almost relieved. After all I'd never landed a basking shark and God knows how Mum had struggled with a two-pound mullet.

As the line began to tighten, the monster was again stirred into action and took off for what appeared to be at least another twenty lengths. Since the sages and I were probably only eleven or twelve with fairly undeveloped right arms, the rod was passed between us until each in their turn tired and passed the rod as if in a relay race. Another couple of years and a few girlie magazines and we'd have had that monster on the bank in five minutes.

After us all having one or two turns at the helm, the rod returned to me, and the sages suggested that I go on the offensive, whatever that meant. The monster had tired (and it was nearly teatime) so we thought it was a good time to have a look. I pulled the rod up and wound the slack in just as if I were fighting a mighty marlin in the Caribbean off the back of a great gin palace. For what seemed like hours I slowly heaved the monster up from the depths and, while he occasionally made a heroic dash and took back a few yards, I think we both knew that he was beaten. The line straightened as the fish came underneath us and the sages peered over my shoulder into the clear water to get a first glimpse of this now subdued silver torpedo.

The incredible colour was the first thing that struck me, as silver as a new fifty-pence piece with a brilliant white under his mouth, a dorsal as big as my hand, and massive great nearly-transparent pectoral fins. We didn't really know at the time, but this was our first encounter with what must be the king of all fishes, the Atlantic salmon, more commonly known to us local nippers as a smoothie.

We somehow managed to get the smoothie out of the water and onto the bank, although I can't think how because we didn't possess a landing net, nor did we know anything about tailing salmon. It horrifies me now to think of how we killed that beautiful fish, and probably goes some way to explaining why I am now so passionate about catch and release.

We headed back home across the reed marshes with our now dead smoothie, to what we felt would surely be a hero's welcome from our admiring parents. We were at least an hour late for tea, but what an excuse we had. There was no need to collaborate stories on the way home this time, and I was already imagining the homecoming. Perhaps I would stay quiet for a couple of minutes and take the telling-off from my Mum, which would only exaggerate my moment of triumph when I finally produced the trump card.

As it was, the sages and I fought for the right to carry our prized possession on the final leg of what had turned into a smoothie-carrying relay. I was, as the actual assassin, eventually elected to be the carrier on the glory leg and the pace quickened considerably as we neared the finishing line of my back garden. Of course the timing and the patience went to pieces and we were shouting for attention long before we got into the garden, fighting for position to be the first to break the news of our heroism.

Mum opened the door and looked with an expression that I had never seen before, nor since, and I can only imagine must have been similar to that of a first time father who momentarily glances at the dangerous end during childbirth. It was a combination of amazement, wonderment, disbelief and shock—plenty of shock. Mum, without saying anything, slowly shut the door, gathered her thoughts, and then opened it again. The same expression reappeared, although the door this time remained open, as did Mum's mouth.

After what seemed like half an hour of not knowing whose turn it was to talk, Mum came out with the legendary Mum's question:

"Where the bloody hell did you get that from? And more to the point, what on earth am I going to do with it?"

It wasn't what we'd expected, although perfectly understandable considering that our only donation to the menu, to that point, had consisted mostly of grey mullet with the occasional slob trout as a special treat.

After Mum had sat down for awhile, and the sages and I had run through the sequence of events—all speaking together, and getting louder and louder and faster and faster, I think she began to realise the enormity of the task facing her in the cooking of a twenty-six pound fish in an oven which was not quite big enough to warm its tail fin.

Within a few minutes we were all sat around the table eating Marmite on toast and reliving the afternoon's events while Mum pondered exactly what to do with the smoothie. She explained to us that perhaps she was not in the best position to cook the fish and suggested that one of my friend's dads would be the man to offer advice. Mum looked mightily relieved when we agreed that this was a good idea, and so we set off on another parent startling exercise.

At my friend's house the initial reaction was similar although in a slightly more professional way, and before we really knew what was happening we were getting into the car and speeding off into Southampton. There was an air of confusion as we were driven at speed—or as fast as a Hillman Avenger will go—to the back of the Polygon hotel, a very posh facility in the middle of Southampton.

We were instructed to stay in the car while our self-appointed representative, my mate's dad, ventured up to the tradesman's entrance, ridiculously trying to conceal the smoothie under his coat. A rather small, smartly dressed man with a Hitler-style moustache opened the door and looked suitably impressed when the coat was slowly opened to reveal the offering. He disappeared back into the hotel and after a few minutes returned with another, much bigger man dressed all in white with a tall white hat. He was, we concluded, to conduct negotiations on behalf of the hotel. We watched, kneeling on the seat and peering through the back window of the Hillman Avenger as proceedings commenced between our representative—my mate's dad—and the man in the white hat. We kept a steady eye on our smoothie, whose head we could just see hanging from the bottom of our representative's coat.

After discussions lasting a few minutes, the coat was flung open and the smoothie passed to the man in the hat. The small man, who had been lurking in the background, now stepped forward and handed something to our representative, who immediately turned and began walking back to the Hillman.

We quickly sat back down as if we had just witnessed something sinister, something that small boys didn't need to know about, and we tried to act innocently as my mate's dad got back in the car. We calmly asked him what had happened. He didn't say anything; he just started the car and sped away as if he were leaving the scene of a crime.

As we left the hotel car park, I watched as our silver tourist disappeared through the back door of the Polygon Hotel at about the same time as the American variety were entering the front. No doubt they would meet over dinner.

The journey home was conducted as much of the day had been, in a confused silence, all of us desperate to know answers to muddled questions. Number one: where the hell was our smoothie? Why was that man wearing a tall white hat? And when was my mate's dad ever going to explain the stupid grin that had been fixed on his face since we'd left the Polygon?

When we got back to Testwood my mate's dad produced a handful of banknotes from his pocket and carefully counted them out in front of the sages and myself. The counting stopped at sixty pounds.

Sixty bloody pounds!

We were all paperboys earning seventy-five pence per week plus twenty-five pence per extra round. Sixty pounds was an impossible amount to imagine.

Catch and release has a lot going for it, but three year's money for one afternoon's adventure wins every time. Innocence, I'm afraid, was lost and from then on it was every paperboy for himself. For the next few weeks we stood amidst piles and piles of undelivered *Southern Evening Echoes* as we discussed and schemed our transformation into semi-professional salmon fishermen.

We actually caught very few fresh salmon in the weeks after, but we more than made up for it with spawned-out kelts which used to come down the river in their hundreds. They were of course very easy to catch, being either nearly dead, dead, or very dead. It made no difference as to their state of health, however, as our makeup department could perform miracles. First we would take their eyes out, which had normally turned white and looked very unappealing. We would then file off their kypes and scrub them down with Fairy washing-up liquid (lemon scented), which worked wonders on restoring their silver gleam.

After a few unsatisfactory visits back to the Polygon with our scrubbed-up offerings, we deduced that the man in the tall white hat knew a little more about salmon than we'd at first given him credit. We needed a new, less discerning market and the local pub, suitably called The Salmon Leap, was the obvious choice. We soon learned that men leaving a pub, a little worse for wear, and probably in trouble with the wife, made excellent sales targets. In their mind, a nice big salmon seemed a suitable alternative to a bunch of flowers or a box of chocolates as a gift for an angry wife.

As market research goes, we were way ahead of our time.

I think that most of our customers were too embarrassed to question us the next day. Some probably ate the fish without knowing, although it's fair to say we didn't get many repeat orders.

My own advice to anyone buying salmon is to never, ever, buy a fish from anybody near a pub or indeed associated with a pub, as your judgement may be impaired. Secondly, never buy a salmon, or any other fish for that matter, that is missing its eyes. A lot can be learnt of the state of a fish's health, or more importantly how long it's been dead, through the appearance of its eyes. Thirdly and most importantly, never under any circumstances buy a salmon with even the faintest hint of lemon washing-up liquid about it.

Two Men in a Boat

I left school in 1979 at age fifteen with mixed feelings of relief and excitement. I was keen to quickly get a job and earn some money to pay for what I had long dreamed of doing; travelling the world.

Through a friend of my Dad, I was offered work as a trainee yacht-rigger inside an old railway carriage at Redbridge alongside the Test estuary. I wasn't a yachtsman, but the job sounded very exciting and the potential for travel was certainly appealing. Much of the work was fairly mundane, although jobs onsite added a certain sparkle and my mates thought I was glamorously employed. I was paid the princely sum of twenty-eight pounds per week, of which I happily gave Mum five pounds per week for housekeeping. Living at home allowed me to save most of my salary, apart from what I spent on a few pints of boiler down at the Red Lion Pub, and one or two disastrous investments in motorbikes and women, neither of which paid dividends.

When I was eighteen Mum handed me a savings book into which she had paid all of the housekeeping money, which by that time I had very generously upped to eight pounds a week. It was a lump sum of about six hundred pounds, a substantial amount and certainly enough to think about my travelling ambitions.

The first opportunity to broaden my horizons came in October 1981. A boat owner that I met through my yacht-rigging job asked me to help him take his beloved thirty-foot green fibreglass sailing yacht from Hamble to Gibraltar and then possibly on to the Mediterranean. The trip would take us across the English Channel to the western coast of France. From there we would sail across the Bay of Biscay toward the northwest point of Spain. After following the coast of Portugal, a southeast turn would take us to the Straits of Gibraltar.

I was off to see the world, or so I thought.

Within hours of taking this job, I suspected that I may have signed on to an ill-fated expedition. The "captain," I soon learned, knew very little about sailing, yachts, or water in general. How we negotiated our way out of the Hamble River was a miracle in itself and I should have jumped ship there. The weather was atrocious, although in hindsight there's no doubting we would have been in trouble in a flat calm.

Our first stop-off point was, for some strange reason, Yarmouth, on the Isle of Wight. After some well-earned recuperation (it's a long way across The Solent Sea, a gruelling voyage of at least six miles) we headed for our next port of call, Christchurch, which was another ten-mile slog through cold and rough seas. After that leg I remember thinking that it was going to take a bloody long time to reach warmer climates.

This strange hopping along the coast continued until Falmouth where we rested up in preparation for an almost inconceivable attempt at crossing The English Channel. It was while we were in Falmouth that the owner of the boat let slip that he was still learning the ropes on the navigating side of things. He explained that whilst he could still see land, he couldn't be lost, hence his employment of the coastal-hugging tactics. With this new piece of information taken on board I can't say that I was particularly keen on a Channel crossing. Even I knew, with an unquestionably limited amount of experience, that the solid bit of land was unfortunately absent between England and France.

Again, when we left Falmouth, the weather was almost storm force and at all times the phrase "suicide mission" was on the tip of my tongue. But off we went, an apprentice yacht rigger and a useless captain in his crappy little boat, into the teeth of a howling gale, knowing full well that as soon as we lost sight of land we were well and truly in the shit.

Looking back at that day, with visibility at about thirty metres, I think that we were probably in the shit before we reached the end of the marina pontoon. I can remember that the harbour was full of sheltering fishing boats and sizeable trawlers, and that sailing past them, with their incredulous stares and mocking hand gestures (similar to waving, but not quite) should really have made us question the wisdom of venturing further than the harbour walls. However, we fools were off, and there was quite obviously nothing that was going to stop us, other than hitting something, which likely wouldn't take long.

I can't really remember much about the crossing other than having my eyes closed a lot. For all I know the useless captain may have had his eyes closed as well, and if so it wouldn't have mattered as we seemed to have very little control over the boat. After about twenty hours in the pitch black of night, we saw lights which we presumed to be land, although without getting close enough to hear which language the people spoke, there was no way of telling whose land it was. Hopefully the lights were in France, although I wouldn't have been totally surprised to see those same Falmouth trawlers with their mocking hand gestures. The useless captain seemed to regain confidence and decided to head for the lights. I agreed with his call; if nothing else we'd at least run up on the beach where I could escape.

It turned out that the lights were a little further away than we had anticipated, and after several hours we began to doubt that it was land at all. There's every chance that we were following an oil tanker up the English Channel—assuming, that is, that we were actually in the English Channel. Eventually we became aware of the sound of breaking surf and could see the white tops of the waves as they crashed onto the shoreline. I don't know if I was pleased or not, although I did feel resigned to the fact that our voyage was about to come to an end.

After following the shoreline for a few miles we saw some fishing boats moored in a small inlet and decided that this would be as good a place as any for what I presumed would become our final resting place.

The breaking waves catapulted us into the tiny harbour, completely out of control. Standing on the heaving foredeck and trying to grab a mooring line was impossible. The first obstacle that slowed our approach was a line of small fishing boats that were moored in neat rows alongside a line of buoys. We hit most, if not all of them, and the sickening sound of splintering fibreglass echoed around the tiny harbour as we bulldozed our way in.

When our keel finally lodged on the bottom, the boat was knocked on her side by the massive waves crashing into our beam. I was too scared to cry, and I was thinking about which direction I might swim if I launched myself into the melee. The boat rolled onto its side after each wave smashed into our hull, and returned to even keel while waiting for the next one. During one of the more upright moments I let off a distress flare, although the word 'distress' was something of an understatement. I am not a religious person, in fact I am almost anti-religious and blame it for the majority of the world's problems, but what happened over the next five minutes would have made even a hardened atheist wonder. Our keel popped free of the bottom and the boat came upright and seemed to settle just long enough for me to grab a buoy and secure lines fore and aft. Instead of being smashed against the rocky wall of the harbour, we appeared to be moored up.

We had been washed to the back of the little harbour, through most of the fishing boats and mooring lines, and we found ourselves in a relative calm. As we sat in the cockpit not really knowing what to do and trying to understand what had just happened, cars began to arrive and people gathered on the harbour walls and began looking down, trying to find the origin of the distress flare. They were too far away to talk to and no attempt was made to communicate, we just sat there relieved and embarrassed. Our would-be saviours just stared and pointed at us, shaking their heads in confusion. I was thinking of shouting over to them and asking whether we were in France or Ireland, but thought that it was perhaps not the best time.

In the morning, more locals turned up as word spread of these strange invaders who had parked a boat in their harbour. They didn't appear to be laughing or mocking, they just seemed confused.

It must have been almost lunchtime before we finally began to move about. I think it dawned on us that we weren't going to suddenly wake up and realise that it had all been a bad dream. Throughout the day our audience grew into a sizeable crowd, most going home for lunch but quickly returning in case we tried another impromptu manoeuvre.

It appeared that we had wiped out the majority of this small town's fishing fleet. Some of the boats had sunk, and those that remained afloat were moored in a tangled bundle towards the back of the harbour.

It was apparent that our own boat had suffered fairly serious damage, as the sound of water could be heard lapping at the floorboards. It dawned on me that we would have to ask our perturbed audience for assistance, although we considered waiting for dark, slipping our moorings, and gate-crashing somebody else's harbour.

So there we sat, like Christians waiting for the lions to be let in. What had started out as an exciting adventure from the Hamble to the Mediterranean had seemingly finished in a small harbour in either France or Ireland, we still weren't quite sure.

The impasse was finally broken at about two o'clock in the afternoon when a small launch edged towards us with four very official looking people in it. They weren't exactly waving a white flag, but they did appear nervous as they approached this English battering ram which had single-handedly wrecked their local economy.

It turned out that the party of officials was made up of a

customs agent, a policeman, the local sailing club representative, and the local vicar. Were they planning to bury us at sea? They very gingerly came alongside, insisting on mooring themselves, and climbed on board with rather forlorn expressions on their faces. They looked and smelt French but it wasn't until they spoke that we finally knew in whose country we'd caused so much destruction. Needless to say, neither the useless captain or myself spoke a word of French although in a rather embarrassed attempt at breaking the silence I did try the sentence I most remembered from lessons at school.

"Jean Paul et Marie dans le jardin avec le chien?"

Unfortunately that didn't seem to help much, in fact hardly at all. They turned and whispered among themselves and I'm almost certain that one of them referred to me as a "stupid English prick."

It turned out that we had crashed into the small fishing town of Le Conquet on the French coast about twenty miles northwest of Brest. Our passports were carefully scrutinised. Boat registration and insurance documents were also called for and to my amazement the useless captain did seem to have all the relevant paperwork up to date and close at hand.

The atmosphere seemed to improve once they found that our insurance papers were in order. It changed again, however, when they caught sight of the amount of water inside the boat, and they departed rather more quickly than they had arrived.

As they retreated to their launch, they made it clear that we were to go ashore to finalise insurance details, and the sooner the better. It occurred to me that perhaps one of us should stay behind to make sure that our insurance company would not have to pay for more skiffs than we had actually damaged. What was left of their fleet was a bit run down, and a few enterprising saboteurs could easily arrange for a full replacement.

After picking our way through the throng of onlookers on the harbour wall, our warders escorted us to the local police station where all of the legal stuff was sorted out and many phone calls were made to alarmed insurance companies back home. When we returned to the harbour and looked down on our boat from the wall, we got our first view beneath the clear waters, some twenty feet below.

Right then, it became apparent why our spirited midnight arrival had drawn such a curious crowd of onlookers. The entrance to the harbour was very deep, as was the majority of the basin. The rear fifty feet of the harbour, however, had been deliberately cordoned off for the exclusive use of smaller dinghies and it was separated from the deeper areas with the erection of a substantially built man-made wall which came to within three feet of the surface. As it turned out, it wasn't the harbour bottom that grabbed our keel and pitched us onto our side, it was this submerged wall that was designed to discourage boats like ours from entering. This wall was topped with poles and round plastic beacons every five feet or so to warn all fishing boats that this area was for much smaller vessels with drafts of three feet or less. On this morning, however, the area was filled with a smashed and tangled collection of small dinghies, racing buoys, a few rowing boats, five canoes…and one thirty-foot English yacht flying the Royal ensign. No wonder the crowd had been so perplexed.

Bloody English.

Looking down at our carnage, I was relieved that we hadn't attempted a sneaky escape when night fell. Sailing once over a submerged wall in a deep-draft boat was bad enough, twice would have been pushing it.

Once we were back on the boat the general atmosphere of doom and gloom quickly returned and floating bedclothes didn't help the situation. Actually talking to our French pals had been something of a relief, especially once they realised that we were properly insured. At this point, however, the relationship between the useless captain and myself was at a bit of a crossroads. We remained at odds for a few days while we waited for a forty-ton crane to lift us out of the dingy basin for an inspection of our hull and an eventual deposit back into deeper water. After determining that we were no longer seaworthy, temporary hull repairs were made and a towboat was arranged to haul us twenty miles down the coast to Brest where a full survey could be carried out.

On our departure day, the crane dropped us near the harbour entrance and the operator made sure that our bow was pointed toward the open sea before he released the slings. Another large crowd gathered to watch us being towed out of the harbour. The Mayor was there, as were several local dignitaries. There may have been a band, but I'm not sure. I was mightily relieved that we couldn't go under our own steam; who knows where we would have ended up?

At Brest, our yacht was hoisted into a cradle where the damage was assessed and a professional opinion given on work required. As it turned out, the boat needed substantial repair, which would take several months, perhaps longer. The thought of spending another two nights with the useless captain was bad enough, two months was unthinkable. My window for escape was now wide open, so I packed my scant belongings and said goodbye.

A few years later I heard that the captain had sailed the same boat into a whale during a single-handed yacht race, and the boat went to the bottom of the Atlantic. The captain was saved, and I'm hoping that he may have finally realised that perhaps this yacht-racing lark wasn't for him.

After our disastrous voyage I returned to England and my job as a yacht rigger. I was well-bitten by the travelling bug, but from that point forward I would stick to hard, dry terra firma. Over the next few years I thumbed rides across America, and toured parts of Eastern Europe and North Africa via motorbike, but eventually travel lost its glamour and I returned home with a renewed appreciation for quiet riverbanks.

Meeting My Mentor

y Grandad lived alone at Furzehill, a tiny place a few miles from Fordingbridge in the New Forest about half an hour from where I was living. He had once lived in a bungalow with two acres of beautiful gardens, but that eventually became too much for an eighty-five-year-old man to look after. He sold the house but retained a small piece of the garden on which he was granted permission to put a mobile home.

I remember that it had one of those Rayburn fireplaces on which he was told to burn only smokeless fuel. Of course, living in a wooded area and being a forester all of his life, he burnt just about everything but smokeless fuel—in fact, it seemed the smokier it was the more he liked setting fire to it. He also used to smoke a pipe almost non-stop and that only added to the 1920's London atmosphere. Passive smokers would have been moaning, or nowadays suing, for miles around.

He smoked continually from the age of about ten until his death at the grand age of ninety-two. If he wasn't sleeping or eating, he was generally smoking. Of course he was very fit and never had a day's sick in all his working life. He was the epitome of the elderly relative that all heavy smokers trot out in defence of their habit.

One unfortunate side effect of my Grandad's "if it doesn't move, burn it" attitude was that the Rayburn typically glowed with a heat of which any blacksmith would be proud. Most of us, Grandad apart, couldn't get within twenty feet of it. With the smell, the noise, and the intense flames, one could very easily imagine that he was stood on the footplate of the Flying Scotsman charging through the night towards Edinburgh. If you closed your eyes tightly you could even hear the screaming whistle.

Grandad would very often fall asleep in front of the fire, wake up in the early hours and go on to bed (after a final smoke, of course). One day down at Furzehill, a worried Grandad confronted me; he'd lost his slippers and couldn't find them anywhere. After much searching I found them, melted to the top of the Rayburn. He'd fallen asleep with his legs resting on top of the fireplace. When he woke he'd gone to bed and left his slippers stuck to the side of the now cooled inferno. Worrying about him dying from pipe smoking was somewhat pointless.

While I was chiselling his slippers off the fire, I noticed a recent issue of the *Avon Advertiser* on the hearth. The newspaper was opened on an article about a man named Simon Caine who was a split-cane rod maker and who worked on the restoration of chalkstreams. I was utterly engrossed in the article and read it three or four times. This man had managed to build a life and a living around fly fishing and rivers. He was doing the job that my dreams were made of and I immediately knew that I somehow had to contact him. I suddenly became aware of being twenty-six years old and still working in a job in which I had very little interest. This was my chance.

Leaving Grandad to chisel off the other slipper, I sat at the table and wrote a letter to Simon Caine explaining my situation and how interested I was in his work, and could he please give me any pointers on how to get into something similar.

This was January 1988. It all seems fairly naïve now but I was so suddenly immersed in this feeling of knowing exactly what I wanted to do, and it had to be done there and then. I addressed the letter to the newspaper asking them to pass it on to Simon Caine and posted it on the way home from Grandad's.

Two days later I received a reply from Simon, which I still have. In his reply he thanked me for my interest, warned me of the difficulties in getting a riverkeeper's job, and graciously answered all of my naïve questions. On the reverse of the letter he jotted down a couple of addresses who he suggested I contact for further information. Letters were written within the hour and posted to these new contacts, one of which was a fellow named Ron Holloway, a keeper on the famous River Itchen at Martyr Worthy.

The next day, a Saturday, the phone rang at eight in the morning. I remember thinking that Grandad had probably burnt down the New Forest or maybe stuck something a bit more important than his slippers to the Rayburn. Instead, it was Mr. Holloway himself saying he'd received my letter and perhaps I'd like to meet him on the Middle Beat Bridge, in shall we say, half an hour?

After taking down a few directions, I was bombing down the M27 feeling excited, nervous and indeed slightly confused. Within five days of writing a letter to the *Avon Advertiser,* I was on my way to meet a famous riverkeeper of a premier beat on a world-renowned chalkstream.

As I drew closer to our meeting point, I reflected back on the evening prior and cursed that last pint of Guinness and the chicken madras. I wished I had washed before jumping in the car; I looked like a scarecrow, felt half-pissed, and smelt like a curry house. The rest of the journey was spent with the windows wide open, a pathetic attempt to disperse my pungent aroma while my Dad's advice rang in my ears, "It's all about creating a good first impression." It was with nervous apprehension that I parked the car and walked down to the bridge for my meeting.

If you asked any schoolchild to draw what they thought a riverkeeper looked like, each drawing would bear an uncanny resemblance to Ron Holloway. There were deep creases cut into his tanned, leathery skin and you could see that his face had been continually exposed to relentless summer sun and autumn driving rain in equal measure. He had a great handlebar moustache and equally impressive side burns that almost reached his broad shoulders. The middle part of his moustache was a different colour from the rest—a dingy mixed palette of Guinness and Golden Virginia. He loved his tobacco and he could roll a cigarette without looking at it. His eyes were constantly locking on to anything that moved and you'd bet your bottom dollar that he could spot a trout from a great distance on a cloudy day. As he came towards me I can vividly remember thinking, *blimey, he looks worse than I do!*

I immediately liked him.

He shook my hand firmly and welcomed me to Martyr Worthy. I got a definite whiff of both alcohol and curry, although I presumed it was my own breath rebounding of his rather large frame.

"Had a bloody good curry in Arlesford last night," he said with a bloody good curry smile that I would recognise anywhere. "Tad too much to drink, too, a bit delicate this morning."

I almost loved this bloke and we'd only said hello.

Standing on that bridge, smelling of Guinness and curry, looking at the crystal clear water with the great swathes of ranunculus hovering over the polished gravel was my introduction to the River Itchen. I felt a great affinity to the man next to me, not only because he smelt like me, but because of the way in which he pointed things out and explained things to me with such amazing enthusiasm. There was no doubting his passion and love for the river. He must have stood on that spot a thousand times before yet it was still exciting for him. Among the pieces of advice and instruction that he offered that day, was this profound statement of the requisite attributes of the job I was longing to have.

"Donny," said Ron, "there are two things that you need to become a riverkeeper. One is the lack of desire for wealth, and the other, equally important, is a good liver."

We covered many topics standing on the bridge that morning, but once it became established that we shared a love of curry, Guinness, brown trout, blue-winged olives, cricket, and the Southampton Football Club, Ron extended his hand and enlisted my part-time assistance, there and then.

He told me many years later that there would have been a more formal interview process, had the pub not been shut on that particular morning.

Life at Martyr Worthy

ven though I was still working full-time as a yacht rigger, I was
grateful of the rare opportunity that Mr. Holloway afforded.
My time on the river with Ron was limited to evenings and weekends,
but I cherished every moment that I was able to work alongside him.

Apprentice, or "underkeeper" positions are fairly uncommon
and openings are very rarely advertised. There is only a fraction of
the number of riverkeepers that there used to be, mainly because
the toffs haven't got the money they used to, and many of those
jobs are passed from father to son.

There are some excellent colleges in England which offer all
manner of fishery courses, but in this business, unfortunately, a lot
comes down to not what you know, but who you know.

Ron Holloway was an integral part of the news line that travelled up and down the chalkstream valleys; he was a good person
to know. He used to write the Hampshire reports for the *Trout and
Salmon* magazine and many times he would get sharply criticised
for daring to suggest something a little different, or for disagreeing
with some piece of age-old tradition. Those critics, however, didn't
seem to bother him in the slightest; he'd just laugh and carry on

writing. Ron had an incredible understanding of the scientific workings of both the rivers and the fish, and his knowledge and advice was greatly sought after both in this country and abroad.

There weren't many places that you could go with Ron without someone coming up to say hello. He seemed to know thousands of people; or rather they knew him. Many times somebody would approach him in a pub and congratulate him on a piece of writing or lecture that he had given. Those meetings would often result in a lengthy discussion on some fishery or chalkstream matter. Twenty minutes later they'd shake hands and the stranger would go as if leaving a long lost friend. When I'd ask Ron who they were, he'd usually say, "I haven't got a clue, never seen them before."

Ron was of course a wonderful fisherman, and a finer dry-fly angler I have yet to meet. One of the first times with him at Martyr Worthy we were sat alongside the river next to his top beat bridge, drinking whisky with a gentleman who was fishing the evening rise. He was a Canadian chap and a famous fly tier and himself an excellent fisherman. He had a little green bag slung over one shoulder that he was constantly looking into.

Ron was telling him what insects were hatching and what the trout were feeding on. On cue the Canadian took this little green bag off his shoulder, carefully moved the whisky to one side, and spread the contents onto the wooden table. At first it wasn't obvious exactly what the contents were but after a little adjusting and screwing the odd piece together, a fly-tying vice was clamped to the table and a little net was assembled. The Canadian took the net and walked onto the bridge. After a few moments of carefully observing the surface film, he scooped up some of the naturals that the trout found so irresistible. He walked slowly back to the table studying his catch which he then proceeded to transfer into a small test tube which he stood on the table in front of us. Within five minutes of deathly silence in which even the captured olive seemed fascinated, the Canadian had tied an exact replica, a mirror image.

The Canadian passed the fly on to Ron, who quickly tied it onto his leader. Ron stepped into the river, spotted a rising fish, and after one or two false casts the fly landed like thistledown eighteen inches upstream of his target. As the fly drifted down over the trout the tension became unbearable and the Canadian and me gulped our whisky at the same time. My eyes were still watering as the imitation was taken and I jumped, as I still do, on most dry fly takes.

Ron played the jumping little wild brownie for a few moments and released it back to the river. He walked slowly back to the table, poured a healthy quota of whisky into each of our glasses, and sat down again with a quietly self-satisfied grin.

After a long silence, he turned to me and calmly said, "Observation, imitation, and presentation." That was, and still is to me, what trout fishing is all about.

How I didn't burst into a round of spontaneous applause I shall never know.

Ron taught me an endless amount about chalkstream management during my apprenticeship. The hardest work on the Martyr Worthy beat was undoubtedly the sub-surface weed cut, of which there were four each year: May, June, July and October.

The June cut was usually ten days and was started at seven o'clock on the first day and finished late on the tenth day. It was incredibly hard work and I have never seen as prolific a weed growth as occurred at Martyr Worthy. Some days you would be cutting for twelve hours, moving literally tons of weeds from the river, yet come the end of the day you could hardly see where you'd been. Of course, all of the weed was cut with a hand scythe and after three or four days your arms felt ready to drop off.

Once the cut was finished, the river would look absolutely beautiful and all the hard work seemed worthwhile, but believe me, it started growing back almost as quick as you could cut it.

There is a tremendous art to weed cutting, to do it properly takes great skill and the reason that the weed growth was so prolific at Martyr Worthy was mainly due to the way in which it was cut by Ron and his predecessors. The amount of weed that we'd cut varied upon the amount of water in the river and no two cuts were ever the same. Some of the July cuts were little more than a trim up, while in October we would hit everything hard. This ensured that none of the weed root structure would be lost during any winter flooding and also enabled any build up of silt to be moved on.

Other than the hectic weed cuts, life for me at Martyr Worthy was fairly relaxed and I would spend most of my time listening and learning from Ron. If the river was up together and no fishermen about, at dinner time we would usually go to his office, or The Chestnut Horse as other people called it, and sample a few of the local ales.

Ron and his wife Paula both make some of the best curry I've ever tasted and although they have given me all the recipes, mine never seems the same. Many times we would have curry for tea, and then we'd jostle for position with the five spaniels next to the fire. The dogs would get so close to the fire that you could smell their coats burning but they wouldn't dare move and risk losing position. After four pints of Bass down at the Chestnut Horse, homemade curry, and five smouldering spaniels, the smell must have been delightful. I always wondered why Paula spent so much time sat in the kitchen.

Ron was also a casting instructor and must have taught thousands of people how to cast, me included. He taught me in the same place that he taught others, in the horse paddock behind his house; I spent many hours there casting at daisies and buttercups.

A slow pick up to ten o'clock, quicken to twelve, and pause. Back to ten and a slow return to rod tip down. Totally effortless, let the rod do the work, no power required—just timing. You know when you've done a good cast the minute you start the forward movement. You've paused long enough and just feel the bite of the line, you know the line is going to come from behind your head and lay in an arrow straight line on the grass in front of you. Try as I might, I cannot explain to my wife how I can gain so much pleasure from casting a straight line in the middle of a field.

Ron taught me well and I hope he is pleased when he watches me fish, although he still likes to make a few comments and suggest one or two improvements. "Too much power Donny, stop looking at the bloody line, you're going past the vertical. Keep at it though, you're getting better. Another ten years or so and I reckon you'll be pretty good!"

Thanks for everything Ron, especially the curry.

The Undertakers

ithin two years of taking the apprentice job at Martyr
Worthy, I found myself with a new wife and a hefty mortgage. I was twenty-eight years old and while juggling two jobs was
tiring, there was no way that I could yet afford to walk away from my
yacht-rigging work. I was well paid and at times the work was great
fun. I met some wonderful people that owned beautiful yachts but I
knew that it was not my long-term career. My time with Ron Holloway
reinforced the notion that riverkeeping was in my blood and working
at Martyr Worthy provided me with the light at the end of the tunnel.

Within five years we had added three children to the mix
and at that point I began searching for a permanent job as a riverkeeper. To pack up and change careers must have seemed to many
at the very least irresponsible, if not a little selfish; but my wife, Jo,
was full of encouragement and without her support I would likely
still be rigging yachts.

My first real chance of a keeper's job was in 1997 at Broadlands on the lower Test. As you can imagine, having waited for so
long I was very excited about the possibility of working on such a
famous chalkstream beat. I had one or two very friendly interviews

with the estate managers and then a tour of the river with the head keeper, Bernard Aldrich. He told me that there had been nearly eighty applicants who had been whittled down to a remaining three, who then had to face a final interview with the land agents.

In basic terms, land agents act as the grossly overpaid link between wealthy estate owners and the common man who works their land. On matters of personnel and estate management, they bridge the gap between these two disparate classes of people, thereby cutting out the necessity of awkward direct communication between "His Lordship" and the riverkeeper.

I can talk to riverkeepers all day long and after working with Ron for a few years I felt fairly confident in my abilities. I soon learned, however, that these agents are not interested in your knowledge of keeping; they're more interested in your people skills. They want to know how you would deal with the rich and famous and how you would cope with difficult fishermen.

I had to go to a posh hotel in Romsey for the meeting with the land agents, and as I was led into an interview room I found myself stood in front of three rather dour looking men. None of them made eye contact and my deliberately fixed and confident smile was therefore wasted.

This time I had actually spent a bit of time washing and dressing for the interview, but they obviously had not. I arrived done up like a dog's dinner but these three looked like they'd just nailed down a coffin lid in a 1930's undertaker's office. As I settled uneasily into the chair, there was no smiling or welcoming, just a straight cold stare which seemed to pass right through me.

They introduced themselves, but at such speed that I didn't catch any of their names. I was nervous, but I felt prepared for the interview and was ready for anything that they threw at me. The middle one cleared his throat and prepared to fire off his first question.

"What action would you take if one of your paying rods—let us say a wealthy, well-to-do-lady—had a little too much to drink and told you to fuck off?"

Unfortunately it was a question that I hadn't given much

thought to, and I remember thinking that perhaps reading up on the history of the Mountbatten family may have been a waste of time. As the sweat prickled onto my forehead I wrongly thought that maybe this was the time to give an amusing answer.

"Well…if she had already given me my tip…then I probably would…just…fuck off."

I can't be sure, but I think the undertaker on the right briefly smiled. The other two glanced down at their paperwork with life-less scowls to remind themselves of my name so they could quite deliberately put a long pencil line right the way through it when the interview ended.

The rest of the meeting felt like a waste of time, and it wasn't long before I was walking back to my car and taking what I knew would be a last look around the beautiful Broadlands estate.

Needless to say, the letter I received from them the following week contained the expected sad news, but then I don't suppose they do a funny one.

A few months later another opportunity came up at the Houghton Club, again on the Test, and possibly the most famous of all chalkstream beats. Of course, I quickly applied.

I went through exactly the same procedure as with the Broad-lands job with an interview, a tour of the beat with the head keeper and then both Jo and myself were shown around the house and given another tour. Well, we had virtually picked out the wallpaper, decided which school our children would attend, and basically sat back and waited for the job offer. A letter duly arrived informing me that the significant numbers of applicants had now become a shortlist of three. It was beginning to sound a little familiar and perhaps a little too similar to previous attempts. The letter went on to invite us to a final interview with the land agents who would be representing the Houghton Club.

Oh, bollocks. I only hoped that the Houghton Club employed different undertakers than Broadlands did.

Although the interview with the Houghton land agents was marginally better than the first one, I wasn't offered that job either.

Ron and I spent a lot of time discussing my future career, usually while drinking Bass down at the Chestnut Horse. He always told me to keep looking and a full-time riverkeeper opportunity would one day come along. I knew he was right, one *would* eventually come along; what I was worried about was the bloody land agents that might come along with it.

Nursling

orking with Ron Holloway meant that I had direct access to the chalkstream hotline that travelled the length of the Test and Itchen valleys with all manner of gossip, scandal and most importantly, job vacancies. Ron knew which keepers were coming up for retirement, or possibly moving away, and he introduced me to many riparian owners and land agents responsible for appointing underkeepers.

One of those was the leaseholder at Testwood, which I still regarded as my home water. In October of 1997, the leaseholder contacted Ron asking if he knew of anybody able to lend a hand with some fringing and general work at Nursling, which had now become a sister beat to the Testwood water. Ron gave him my number and we arranged to meet over at the river to see what needed doing. I was living in Testwood at the time, which was rather convenient, and I readily agreed to help out for a couple of days. I had seen very little of the river at Nursling before, although I knew of the famous keeper on that beat, Vic Foot.

During my mischievous youth, Nursling was considered out of bounds and the wrong side of the water meadows for us Testwood nippers. Although it was only a half-mile or so away, we only ventured over once. We came over with our rods and bread and started fishing on a little stretch of water we knew to be private. Fishing on new waters was very exciting and although we didn't catch anything we had great fun exploring different parts of the river.

After a couple of hours of fruitless fishing we saw a stranger walking down the banks toward us and we laid flat on the ground probably thinking that if we couldn't see him, he wouldn't see us. Unfortunately his eyesight was better than we had hoped, and while giving us a telling-off he reeled both our lines in and told us we were in big trouble. We stood there apologising and hoping to God that he wouldn't tell our dads.

The stranger told us that we'd have to walk up Mill Lane and see the riverkeeper who would decide our punishment. It seems quite incredible in this day and age that we did actually walk up to see the keeper, but we were too scared not to. Nowadays if I catch any nippers fishing on the river they usually tell *me* to bugger off or they'll tell *their* dads.

When we got to the keeper's cottage he was outside saying goodbye to a couple of fishermen, so we stood in silence, heads bowed, nervously waiting to admit to him that we'd been fishing on his river. As the fishermen drove away he turned towards us and I felt the hairs on the back of my neck stand up in fright. Before either of us had a chance to speak he asked us if we had caught anything, and then he told us to make sure we didn't fish on his stretch of river again—or more importantly, don't get *caught* fishing on his stretch of river again. With that he said goodbye and disappeared into the house waving as he walked through the door. We stood there for a couple of minutes looking at each other not quite knowing what to do. Then the door of the fishing cottage opened again and his head popped out and he asked if there was anything else that we wanted. My mate held up his flask and asked if we could have some water. The keeper came back to the gate, took our flask and disappeared into the house again. A few minutes later he returned with the flask and said that he hoped the water was okay because it tasted a little different down Mill Lane and perhaps we should try it before we left.

We thanked him and said it would be fine and that we really should be getting home. At the bottom of Mill Lane we stopped and opened the flask, which he had filled with beautiful cold orange juice. I can remember standing there, many years ago, drinking orange juice and thinking what a kind thing to do and what a lovely man. That was my first encounter with my second riverkeeping guru, the legendary Vic Foot.

———

I arranged to meet the leaseholder at the fishing cottage at Nursling, so that I could collect the keys to the shed and help myself to the tools I'd need for the fringing work. When I arrived at the cottage he wasn't there, so I had a look around the overgrown garden and the outside of the house, which had obviously been empty since Mr. Foot had retired a few years earlier. In my mind I could still see Vic standing in the doorway saying goodbye to his fishermen and glancing down at two wide-eyed nippers holding fishing rods behind their backs. The whole scene seemed to have been frozen in time and abandoned to nature.

I worked a couple of days for the leaseholder, fringing the banks and clearing the pathways and was immediately bewitched with the Nursling beat. It's a fantastic piece of water with mill pools, shallows, and deep runs. The most delightful stretch, called the Little River, spurs off the main Test and finds its own way to the estuary. It's more like a beat from the top of the Test, with polished gravel and prolific growths of ranunculus.

A week or so after I finished the day-work at Nursling, I was phoned up by the leaseholder and asked if I would be interested in working there full time. I couldn't believe what I was hearing. I sensibly told him that I'd have to think about it.

"Yes, okay, then!"

After so many years of apprenticeship, I was finally going to work as a full-time riverkeeper—and on a fabulous stretch of the Test, only minutes from where I'd grown up. At that point, I could only think of Ron Holloway and my wife, Jo, who had encouraged me to incessantly follow my dream.

We moved into the fishing cottage on January 1, 1998 and I cannot describe what an exciting day that was. The house had been empty for some time, and smelled damp and musty. My Mum and Dad had spent the previous few days cleaning the carpets and Jo's parents helped with the moving of what seemed like tons of our belongings. I spent much of the day wandering about the garden, looking all around the house, not quite believing that I was actually going to be living there. I walked down to the river and wandered around the legendary Drawing Room Pool at the top of the Little River, opposite my house. *My house*…it was incredible. I didn't help much with the moving.

On my first Monday at Nursling, I finished my breakfast, walked outside, and found myself with no idea of what I was supposed to do. For the first time in many years, I had nobody to tell me to cut grass or fringe banks.

Wow…responsibility.

I decided, first, that I should familiarise myself with my new beat, walk the entire spread, and get to know the water. I walked through the gate onto the riverbanks as my wife waved to me from the window. I felt like a kid on his first day going to a new school.

Nursling is a beautiful beat with fantastic fishing on some superbly varied water. During the late summer when the water is crystal clear, the river becomes an aquarium with an astonishing array of species. The bottom end of the Little River is tidal and attracts lots of sea fish as well as the standard river fish. I have seen twenty-pound carp laid alongside seabass. Pike in the same pool as salmon, bream, mullet and chub. It truly is an amazing piece of water.

The Nursling beat consists of about a mile and a half of the main River Test and the entire length, about two miles, of the Little River Test. Most of the main river is stocked with brown trout of about two pounds and is fished with dry flies only. The remainder of the main Test and the Little River are not stocked, and are fished for seatrout and salmon.

I walked upstream along the Little River to where it spurs off the main River Test and sat on a wooden seat alongside a beautiful pool called Lock Hatches. From my seat I could look straight up the main river and see the motorway that is almost the boundary between Nursling and Broadlands. It was about half past seven on a Monday morning and the traffic was at an almost standstill. It was a beautiful crisp January day with a brilliant blue sky and a slowly rising sun burning off the last of the morning mist.

All I could hear was the water bubbling through the hatches into the pool and a constant cawing from magpies hunting in the surrounding trees. The tail of the Lock Hatches pool suddenly erupted as an absurdly large salmon leapt from the depths and belly-flopped back into the water. I looked back upstream towards the motorway at the traffic, wondering where all those people were going, or were not, whatever the case. Great white clouds of exhaust fumes rose into the sky. The steamed up windows, the blaring radios, the frustration, the usual Monday morning parked on the motorway going nowhere fast.

I stood up and looked at the ripples spreading across the pool where the salmon had landed. I was in the right place. This is what I had always wanted to do, what I had worked for, what I had travelled for, it had all led to this. It was the opening of a new chapter in my life. I turned my back on the packed motorway and walked downstream through the dew-covered grass to explore more of my beat.

On that first day, I reckon I must have walked about thirty bloody miles.

The Legendary Vic Foot

ne afternoon during my first week at Nursling, I was lifting some of our belongings into one of the garden sheds when a voice called out to me. As I came out of the shed to see who it was, I caught his eye and once again felt the hairs stand up on the back of my neck.

"Hello, you must be the new man," he said. "Me mate's cats still live 'ere; wondered if you'd mind still feeding 'em for us?"

I hadn't seen Vic for more than twenty years but he'd not changed a bit. After shaking hands and him talking for fifteen minutes, I asked him if he'd like a drink and he came into the house—the house that he'd lived in for a half century. He sat down and I made him a cup of tea with a slug of whisky in. As I placed it in front of him I just couldn't resist saying, "Have a sip first, Vic, apparently the water tastes funny down Mill Lane."

Vic became a welcomed and regular visitor, and once while he was in the house having a cup of tea he asked if he could use the toilet. Without thinking I said, "Of course, it's up the stairs, first door on the right." I froze with embarrassment, hoping that he wouldn't be offended.

"Donny" said Vic, "I reckon on average I have ten craps a week. That's five hundred and twenty craps a year. In forty-eight years, that's twenty four thousand nine hundred and sixty craps. I know where the bloody toilet is."

When I first started at Nursling it was a bit off-putting when people's first question was always, "How's Vic?" After ten to fifteen minutes worth of Vic stories, they would then ask, "How about you, Donny, things going well?"

It doesn't take long to understand the incredible respect for Vic among chalkstream anglers and it's quite impossible not to love him. Through his kindness and knowledge of the Nursling beat, my introduction to keeping on the Test was made much easier.

Early on, I found that advising experienced Nursling fishermen was quite difficult for a relatively young, new keeper. Consoling dejected anglers was also tough, especially since I was still trying to learn the differences between salmon and seatrout. After one particular morning of almost constant moaning from a disconsolate fisherman, there was a look of relief on his face as Vic walked into the house at dinnertime.

"Why aren't I catching anything, Vic?" said the fisherman, with a look at me that said, *listen and learn sonny, the master will sort us out.*

"Well sir, one of two reasons. Either there's no fish in the river, or it could be that you're just a useless fisherman."

Vic has taught me many things about the Nursling beat, more importantly, though, he taught me a lot about how to treat the rods, the relationship between the keeper and the fishermen. Vic treats everybody the same: the rich and the famous, lords and ladies, scaffolders and bricklayers.

Many times I have been sitting in the fishing lodge listening as Vic begins to tell stories to some wealthy aristocrat. Invariably I end up nearly sinking beneath the table thinking, *not the lesbian joke, Vic, please not the lesbian joke.* But of course he tells it and they always end up in fits of laughter. He gains a lot of respect for what some seem to think are old-fashioned values; his honesty and innocent outlook on life are a big part of his charm.

I remember two fishermen who were fishing Nursling for the first time and who were more excited about meeting Vic Foot than about the actual fishing. They were staying in Romsey and they asked Vic directions to a certain hotel.

Vic replied in his beautiful, deep Hampshire accent, "Now then let me see. Turn down the road where the post office used to be and then turn again. My uncle used to shoot pigeons in the meadow, there. Carry on down the road near to where Keith keeps his cattle and go to the right. When my uncle used to shoot the pigeons in the field where the post office was, they used to bet on them. Right, let's see, go to the left and go along to the gravel pits—although they're not there now, but where they used to be, and move to the right and about fifty yards turn left. Then you'll turn right, and…"

After about ten minutes of this, with the fishermen looking totally bewildered, Vic abruptly said goodbye, winked at me and left. The fishermen were completely charmed by Vic and they chattered excitedly of how pleased they were to have finally met him. After singing his praises, they rather sheepishly turned to me and quietly asked, "When we go out of this gate, do we turn left or right?"

I still see Vic at least twice a day, and we spend a lot of time together drinking tea and talking about the river, the fish, and the Nursling anglers. Someone once said that maybe one day I would be known as the Nursling keeper; but after fifty-six years under his eye, I think this will always be Vic's beat. I'd like to believe that one day I'll be as well-known, but I somehow doubt that I'll still be keeping when I'm ninety-two. I'm fortunate to have this job, and to have such a wonderful mentor. I might one day be able to look after the Nursling beat as well as Vic has, but I shall never be able to replace him.

The Northampton Mafia

at Fox, an old keeper on the Itchen, once gave me a bit of invaluable advice on how to interact with anglers: see everything, hear everything, and say nothing. The relationship between the rods and the keeper has without doubt mellowed over the last thirty years, mainly due to a changing clientele. The days of doffing your cap, bowing and scraping, have now thankfully been replaced with a more friendly shake of the hand and a, "Nice to see you again, fancy a cuppa?"

That's not to say there are no secrets to be kept or plenty of discretion to be shown. I'm quite sure that many keepers have seen plenty over the years that they thought best to forget about—and that will never change—although bribes do tend to keep pace with inflation, if not slightly above.

Some of our season rods come a long distance to fish, and a journey of three hours each way knocks a big hole in the day. One of those groups is from Northampton and is affectionately known as the "Northampton Mafia." They all seem to enjoy fishing, but some in the group are more serious about it than others. One thing that they all share is a goal of having a good time. They're partial to spectacular barbecues, and a drink or three, and they really know how to enjoy themselves, although not necessarily just through fishing. It's difficult to cast a fly rod while holding a glass of wine, but they do their best.

On one of their early season visits to Nursling just after I became keeper, it had rained for three or four days before their visit and the river looked something like the Mississippi in flood. Being a little green, I was worried that the Northampton Mafia were going to travel all the way down and be disappointed at not being able to fish. I decided to show a little concern and phoned up a few of them to warn them not to come down. I only managed to get through to two of them (there are eight) and the response from the first was not what I had expected. I told him that the river was un-fishable and to save himself the long journey. He just laughed over the phone and said that he'd see me in the morning. The only other number that I managed to contact wasn't in but his wife answered the phone. I explained the situation and she seemed very pleased and thanked me for my thoughtfulness and told me that she'd gladly pass the message on.

The next day it was still pouring at daybreak, but to my astonishment the Northampton Mafia arrived just as planned. I expected groans of disappointment as they saw the coffee-coloured water, but they appeared to not even notice the river as they came into the fishing lodge and unpacked their food and wine cases. Seven of them had made the trip; the lone missing member, unfortunately, was the one whose wife I had phoned.

They had their usual day of drinking, eating, and laughing, although not a fishing rod was unsleeved. They left quite happily and said they'd see me next time. All eight of them appeared on that next visit, and the one who didn't come the previous time called me aside and asked if he could have a word. I feared I knew what was coming.

"Donny, if the river is ever in flood again, or a coffee colour, or indeed any other colour—or even if some bastard concretes over the river—never, ever, ever, tell my wife that the river is unfishable."

The validity of that point was well made on their next visit in April. It was a cold and bleak day and the river, again, was in poor condition.

Again, they arrived on cue and we went through the steps of chilling the wine and setting up the food. This time they actually unpacked a rod or two, yet none of them seemed to be in a hurry for fishing on such a cold and damp day.

After about an hour sat in the fishing hut drinking wine and smoking, Mr. Butterworth, the head honcho of the Northampton Mafia, slowly rose to his feet and looked out the window at the Drawing Room pool as he let out a long sigh and stretched his arms. I think he was probably weighing up the pros and cons of going fishing for a bit so he could cross that off the list and get back to the real business of the day. He stared out the window for a while and then he sat back down and had another smoke. It did look pretty damp out there.

After a couple more fags, he once again got to his feet and began stringing up his rods. Until he got the fishing bit out of the way, there was no chance of relaxing and getting on with main event.

As we left the fishing hut, me following him like an obedient dog, he suddenly turned around and looked me up and down before asking, "Where's your bloody rod, Donny? You're not just going to stand there watching me make a prick of myself are you?"

Whether he meant to join him fishing or in making a prick of himself I didn't really know, but I went and got my rod just in case.

Mr. Butterworth was fishing with a trout rod of about nine foot and using a salmon fly called an Ally's Shrimp, size eight. The water was quite coloured although you could almost see the bottom. As he had his first couple of casts I sat on the seat alongside the river and readied my rod. It was the first time I had seen anybody fish the Drawing Room pool and I was quite interested to see how he approached it. After half a dozen casts with very slow retrieves, Mr. Butterworth beckoned me over towards him as he slowly edged back from the side of the pool.

"There's two decent fish down there Donny," he said pointing into the pool.

There was nothing obvious as I peered into the murky depths, so I just stared and nodded as if I knew what I was doing. After a bit he had another cast and began a slow figure eight retrieve, mending the line as the fly began to swing into the current. Suddenly the line stopped and he lifted the rod sharply as his reel began to sing. I looked on in utter amazement as Mr. Butterworth's line cut through the water at a quite alarming speed, doing laps of the pool as if a motorcyclist on the wall of death. His trout rod was bent in an extraordinary shape, with the tip appearing to be in contact with the reel that was still screaming in protest. After five minutes we had still not seen the fish, and although it had slowed down a bit, it was still cruising around the bottom of the pool. For a moment I was transported back twenty-five years, standing among the reed beds with the fishing sages wondering what the hell was on the end of our line.

Eventually the fish turned downstream and we followed as it swam out of the Drawing Room Pool. When the fish began to tire it came up for a roll where we caught our first glance of a magnificent smoothie. We eventually got the fish into the net and carefully lifted it onto the bank where the fly fell from its scissors. It was a truly wonderful fish and we estimated its weight at about seventeen pounds. It was on the bank for no more than ten seconds and swam away strongly as Mr. Butterworth and I congratulated each other.

It was my first day with paying clientele (that actually fished) and we'd landed a fantastic salmon, the fish of a lifetime, or so I thought.

As I rang a few people to tell them of our wonderful capture, Mr. Butterworth returned to the Drawing Room Pool where he'd originally spotted the pair of fish. Sure enough, halfway through my second call, I looked up and he was into another one. The same sort of fight ensued, culminating with us sliding a seatrout of about nine pounds in the net. I was absolutely speechless, and remember thinking that this guiding lark was going to be a piece of cake. After the second release, Mr. Butterworth was ready to retire to the lodge and get on with the main business of the day. I hadn't even tied on my fly, let alone cast.

As we sat in the fishing lodge drinking whisky, Mr. Butterworth brought me back down to planet Earth when he told me that in twenty-five years of salmon fishing, this was the biggest he had landed at Nursling—or any other river—and it was also the biggest seatrout he had ever caught. He had fished Nursling hundreds of times and he'd just had his golden half hour, the half hour for which he had waited a lifetime.

I had taken nearly thirty photographs of both captures and was already thinking of presenting him with some of the pictures in a nice frame. When I returned to the house late that evening, a little worse for wear and nudging totally pissed, I ran through the day's events with my wife after thoughtfully waking her up. She didn't appear as excited as me and Mr. Butterworth, but I explained about the pictures, showed her the camera and asked if she could get them developed the next day.

She said that she would, but then she pointed out that getting pictures developed is a little easier if there's a roll of film in the camera.

Alabama:
A Smelly Present From My Brother

fter being at Nursling for a few months, my brother, Christopher, suggested that there was one thing missing. All my thoughts about being a riverkeeper had revolved around the quaint cottage next to the river, my wife making homemade cakes, and a few chickens scratching about in the garden. Even though my wife was never that hot with baking, the rest of that soppy idealism had indeed fallen into place.

As my brother pointed out, however, the obvious missing piece was the faithful riverkeeper's dog, and he wanted to buy me one, in a brotherly kind of way. The only thing that slightly worried me was that while I have always loved dogs, I had never actually owned one, nor lived in a house with one. My brother didn't think it was going to be a problem and said that as long as we went through the right channels and took some advice, we should be all right.

Christopher always does things with great research and detail, and buying a dog was going to be no different. He thought that the wise thing to do was to get some expert opinion, so he phoned the kennel club, who duly recommended some dog selling places. He then set about phoning each kennel and explaining that he wanted to buy a dog for his brother, a newly qualified riverkeeper. As far as what kind or how big we didn't have a clue, just as long as it barked at one end, a stipulation that we thought was fair enough.

One of the kennels that he phoned said that they had just the thing, a failed gun dog that would be perfect company on a river. Naturally, we tried to show a little bit of concern and asked what it had failed on. The owner of the kennel, or gun dog training school as it was, explained that while the dog was of excellent pedigree and a truly wonderful specimen, it was unfortunately scared of pheasants and didn't like gunshot. Even me and my brother, dog novices, could see that these were indeed unfortunate deficiencies for a prospective gun dog. Christopher got the details and the directions to the kennel and we arranged to go and see the dog.

As we pulled into the kennel we were greeted by the deafening din of at least a hundred dogs barking and jumping against the sides of their runs. There seemed to be an awful lot of dogs in a relatively small area that was covered in feces and looked fairly unattractive. It certainly smelt unattractive.

At the back of the kennel we noticed one dog that didn't seem as happy to see us. It was a filthy, skinny, mangy springer spaniel, and my brother and I immediately knew which dog we had come to see.

The owner of the kennel eventually came out, a shady looking man in about the same filthy condition as most of his dogs. As he shook hands I realised it wasn't only his appearance that resembled the dogs, he smelt like them as well.

"I've picked the perfect dog," said the owner, "Let me get him for you."

The man got a couple of scoops of dog food and went into the kennel. The dogs went silent and cowered against the sides of the run as the man filled the bowls with food. As he walked past, the dogs made a mad scramble for the food as if their lives depended on it, which I think they probably did. The mangy dog at the back just sat in the same place in total silence. I began to understand why this one was so skinny and also why all of the dogs were terrified of the shady man.

As he got closer, the dog visibly cowered down until he was almost spread eagled on the floor. The man tied a rope onto his collar and dragged him out. Christopher and I stood watching, and although neither of us knew the first thing about dogs, we both knew what cruelty was, and we both knew that we'd be taking the sad spaniel home with us.

The man brought the cowering dog over to us and apologised for his filthy condition. He said that he had meant to give him a bit of a clean up but hadn't had the time. To the shady man, the dog was just something else to sell, and he spoke about it as if it were a piece of furniture. He told me to take it for a walk and gave me a tennis ball to throw for him. I walked away, not quite knowing what to do, so I just went around the hedge into an adjoining field. The man shouted to let him off the lead and throw the ball for him. I took the piece of rope from the dog's collar fully expecting, almost hoping, that he'd make a dash for freedom and run across the field into the woods. As it was, the dog just sat there looking up at me with a sad expression. There was something in his doleful eyes that told me he was mine, and I think he sensed that things were about to get better for him.

I thought that I'd better go through the motions of looking like a prospective buyer and hurled the ball as far as I could down into the bottom of the field. The dog just sat and looked at me. I looked around to see if I was being watched and then made my way down into the field to get the ball back. As I walked back up the hill I saw that the dog hadn't moved. All right then, so he wasn't that hot on retrieving but by God he was definitely good at staying.

I walked back towards the kennel where Christopher and the shady man stood in uneasy silence, and said that I liked the dog and would be keeping him. The shady man looked genuinely surprised, but invited Christopher, who he recognised to be the payer, into the office to square things up and sort out some paperwork. To this day Christopher has never told me how much this filthy bastard of a kennel owner charged him for my dog, but months afterwards he did tell me that he would have given a thousand pounds if that were the asking price.

Almost as soon as we got home we phoned the kennel club and reported the state in which one of their recommended kennels kept its dogs. Amazingly the kennel club said that it had nothing to do with them. We also rang the RSPCA who said that they had received other complaints and that they would be paying him a visit. We then took the dog to the vet and got him fully checked over. The vet said that the spaniel was suffering from malnutrition and had obviously been poorly neglected. He too wrote letters to the kennel club and RSPCA.

My wife spent many hours cutting all the fur balls out of the dog's ears and grooming and combing him until he looked almost respectable. The vet gave us lots of pills and treatments for him and he slowly but surely began to put on weight and regain his confidence. We found out that he was about eighteen months old and while he already had a name, we decided to change it. I thought back to the time I had spent meandering around the United States, and decided to name him after one place in which I had particularly fond memories. Alabama.

He is now six years old and has turned into a wonderful companion and family pet. We call him "Bama" for short, and I wouldn't change him for the world. He has gone from living in a nightmare to what can only be described as dog heaven.

Christopher has since pointed out what little noise Bama makes, and how that throws doubt on our dog-buying credentials. However, whether he barked or not didn't change the fact that we were now the proud owners of a wonderful dog. Failed gun dog he may be, and scared of those nasty loud bangs and terrifying pheasants, but it doesn't matter. Bama is one of the nicest things that anybody has ever bought me, and on the rare occasion that he actually barks, I immediately think of my brother.

Quality v. Quantity

he disparity of weather, fish behaviour, and angling personalities that I encounter in a typical season means that no two
days on the water are ever the same. Considering all of the variant
psyches, social backgrounds, and motivations for fishing that I see
in a season, I'd have to consider Mrs. Woods and the typical fish-
monger as exact polar opposites.

Mrs. Woods, to me, is the epitome of what dry fly fishing is all
about. The first time I had the pleasure of meeting her was in April
1999, and I was advised by my boss to meet her at the hut, as she
would possibly need some assistance.

I duly turned up at the designated time, not quite knowing what to expect, and anxiously waited for a white car with "at
least one barking dog in it." Exactly on time, a little white Renault
trundled around the gravel track by the side of the mill with a fairly
large collie dog hanging out of the passenger window barking at
nothing in particular. The little car did a seventeen-point turn in
the car park, eventually coming to rest at a chaotic angle. The door
opened and out stepped an elderly woman.

Mrs. Woods is the quintessential English lady, but she has an uncanny coolness about her that occasionally turns dismissive. I remember one day when her dog bit a Frenchman who was sharing the beat with her. An apology was suggested but Mrs. Woods refused. "He's French," she scoffed, "What on earth did you expect the dog to do?"

She is always immaculately turned out when she arrives for her fishing day, though she dresses more for practical purpose than appearance. Mrs. Woods has taught me a lot about dry fly fishing and has always supported my views on over-stocking and the moronic obsession with size of fish.

On a typical day she spends much of her time sat by the river on the Trout Beat and enjoying the peace and tranquillity of the chalkstream. Occasionally she will walk the bank and find a rising fish, and once found she will watch and see what the fish is taking and tie on the appropriate imitation. With equal skill and dexterity, she will cast either left or right handed depending on which bank she is fishing from. Size of the quarry is totally irrelevant and Mrs. Woods will always stick with her initial target, no matter how many fish are rising. She might eventually change from a size 20 to 22, but she'll never leave a rising fish until she either catches it or puts it down. She will only cast upstream and woe betides anyone she sees letting a dry fly drift past them toward the sea. Mrs. Woods treats the whole day as a package deal and only a small amount of that experience actually involves casting a fly. I have never seen her catch more than four or five fish in a day, although she could without doubt empty the river if she were so inclined. On most days she releases every fish, although she will take the occasional one for supper.

Mrs. Woods is a wonderful angler and an absolute joy to spend a day with on the river. Within hours of first meeting her, it became blindingly obvious that there was nothing I could teach her about fly fishing. How to park a car? Well, she could use a bit of coaching, there.

Contrary to Mrs. Wood's meticulous catching of three or four difficult fish in a day, some people come to Nursling solely for the purpose of catching as many trout as possible. During the mayfly hatches, when I wouldn't bet against my spaniel catching a trout on a Grey Wulff, I once had a group of three fishermen who proudly announced that they had caught eighty-seven trout in a single day. When they dropped by the hut at day's end to recount their heroic catch, they looked completely knackered and said that they hadn't stopped all day. Indeed as they were telling me this, they all reached for their rods with glassy-eyed stares, almost subconsciously, as another fish rose next to the hut.

In my eyes, these "anglers" had completely missed the point of what makes fly fishing such a wonderfully challenging sport. They had fished until their arms ached, not daring to stop for lunch in fear of losing valuable casting time and perhaps letting one of their rivals take a fish from their patch while they were resting or having a drink.

They had turned all the fish into numbers: number twelve, number forty-two, and so on. To these men, they weren't fishing for nice brown trout on an idyllic chalkstream; they were bent on racking up a score of numbers on a page—a record that they hoped would surely stand at Nursling for years to come.

I can still picture their dumbfounded expressions when I told them what I thought of their exploits and the damage that I think people like them do to our sport. That's not to say I don't want people to catch fish, I do—and will do all that I can to help them, but I don't like to see people on my beat whose maniacal casting frenzy looks like a helicopter spinning madly out of control. Pick your fish and if you are lucky enough to catch it, then pat yourself on the back, savour the moment, and don't think that a few minutes of non-casting is a waste of time.

Now, with that said, I do fully understand an angler's desire to catch the occasional bigger fish, or his delight in the rare special day where he catches a great number. I'd be quite pompous—not to mention hypocritical—if I bemoaned those pleasures. However, I do feel that there must be some sort of reasonable limit on what an angler should expect from this fishery on a day-to-day basis. I make my opinion on stocking very obvious. We do not stock "trophy" trout at Nursling, nor do I promote this as a "trophy fishery." In fact, the last time I saw a legitimate ten-pounder was in my shopping trolley as I wheeled it up to the supermarket till.

There is a unique tranquillity on the chalkstreams that seems to make the most ordinary of my clientele transcend everyday troubles and suddenly turn into great poets and philosophers. I've seen anglers arrive very quiet and reserved at daybreak, yet come dinnertime they've transformed into sages of incredible wisdom readily giving out free advice on the meaning of life and where it's all going wrong. There are also the few clients that get absolutely rat-faced on the river and make total arses of themselves. I suppose, therefore, that it all balances out in the end, swings and roundabouts.

Some fishermen that visit the Test for the first time are blown away by the sheer tradition of it all and spend much of their time taking photographs. I suppose it would be a bit like getting a pass to walk the pitch at Wembley Stadium, I wouldn't want to play football; merely having a look around would be enough. Other more accustomed rods are often blown away by two or three bottles of a certain red wine and spend most of the afternoon asleep on the riverbank, hoping to wake up for the evening rise.

At the end of the day the fishermen pay good money to fish the chalkstreams and however they wish to spend their time is entirely up to them (as long as they follow the rules and behave relatively well). Sure, we get the occasional fishmongers and trophy-seekers, but rarely do they fish here more than once.

I do wish, however, that we had a few more dry-fly casters as accomplished as Mrs. Woods.

From Nursling to New York

ver the 1999 season at Nursling I counted nearly six hundred anglers that had fished the two beats. Perhaps I should say that nearly six hundred turned up, because not all of them actually fished. Some drank, some barbequed, some slept, and some did other things best not to mention, but nevertheless—they all turned up, in body if not necessarily in mind.

Out of that six hundred I can think of only one that I could quite happily have thrown into the river. Some of the others I wouldn't want to socialise with, but they're fine for a day on the water, and on the whole thoroughly decent people; I'm just glad that they eventually go home when the fishing is over.

On the other hand, there are a few fishermen who have become great friends, and I always look forward to their days at Nursling. One of my favourites is a lovely bloke named John Hackney. John and I have had some great fun salmon fishing together, both at Nursling and in Scotland. I often remind him of the time I caught two salmon after following him through a pool on the River Tweed, and I must say he made a nice job of netting those fish for me. We've had some great times together at Nursling but there was one particular day towards the end of the 2001 season that we shall both remember for the rest of our lives.

John turned up at nine o'clock one morning and we had a hurried cup of tea in the fishing lodge before making our way down the Little River. It was one of those glorious mornings with the first feeling of autumn in the air and heavy dew on the meadows. The sun had begun to lose its summer heat and you could see your breath as if exhaling a good cigar.

Just for one fleeting moment I thought that John would succumb to the occasion and turn his bloody cell phone off, but alas... one step at a time, and he apologised like a naughty schoolboy as it rang for the eighth time, shattering the tranquil silence and echoing across the water meadows.

It's strange, to me, that I can remember almost all of the salmon that I have caught over the years, some with an amazing clarity, yet at times I can't think what day of the week it is, or I'm forgetting birthdays and anniversaries. It is equally strange that I remember very little about the actual fishing from that particular morning, yet I will never forget the events of the day itself.

We had fished our way back up the Little River and were both working our way through the Conegar Pool, which is just the other side of the lane opposite my house. My phone rang and I remember John making some derogatory remark about the ring tone before continuing to roll cast a weighted nymph to the other side of the pool. The call was one of my mates, who asked if I was watching the television and did I think that the world was about to end. He made some strange comment about New York, and suggested we go indoors to watch the news. "And take a bloody great big bottle of whisky with you too," he cautioned.

In a somewhat confused state I told John that we should go and look at the television. He must have sensed that it was something important because he didn't argue my suggestion. Back at the fishing cottage, we turned the television on just as the second airplane slammed into the World Trade Center.

We sat silently and watched the panicked reports as they came across the screen. We watched people throwing themselves from the building to escape the flames. We were still sitting in a numbing disbelief as a million tons of concrete and steel came crashing down and thousands of poor souls perished in a nightmare of apocalyptic scale. We knew that we were witnessing something that would forever change the world, an event that would challenge governments and democracies across the globe.

Could it be that just minutes before I was worried by my choice of nymph or annoyed at a particularly splashy cast?

I could feel sweat running down the middle of my back as I struggled to comprehend the pictures on the television screen in front of me, and the crazy thoughts going through my mind as I searched for an understanding between the days events at Nursling and New York. I remember thinking that perhaps we should have taken our muddy boots off before we came and sat down, but consoled myself in the fact that my wife would surely understand and the telling-off wouldn't be too severe.

Yes sorry about the muddy footprints darling, but we were watching the greatest power on earth being brought to its knees and forgot to take our boots off.

We must have sat there for three hours in bewildered silence staring at the television in a state of complete shock, thinking about those poor people in the planes and on the ground. At almost the exact same moment, John and I looked at each other, let out a long resigned sigh, shrugged our shoulders and made our way back to the river. It wasn't meant to be disrespectful, we just didn't know what else to do.

Flowing waters have this uncanny knack of making the most ordinary of people attempt to become great philosophers. I have heard people say that you will always remember where you were at the time of any great history-changing moment. When democracy was challenged and thousands of innocent people were murdered on that fateful September day in New York, John Hackney and I had been having a wonderful morning fishing the weighted nymph at Nursling.

There are some things that even the river can't help you understand.

A Few Nice Grayling

rayling are a beautiful fish that seem to be coming back into fashion, and on some UK rivers they're now deemed an almost acceptable alternative to the brown trout. They're still viewed as vermin on a few southern chalkstream beats, but on those waters, anything weighing less than five pounds and not waving a white flag like a koi carp is viewed as unfair competition.

I say, Julian, why the disdain for the grayling on your beats?

Well, Roger, they've got that awful hint of cunning and wildness about them.

Yes, yes, old boy. That will never do.

Thankfully the attitude and expectations of anglers have evolved from the days of salmon fishermen hating trout and vice-versa. Most all fish are respected, nowadays, save for the occasional "sport" that still lives and fishes bygone times. After a day of fishing at Nursling, a gentleman once pulled me aside and sharply criticised the amount of coarse fish in the river.

"I was fishing a Red Wulff when this bloody great demon of a chub took it," he said with a snarl, "Damn the foul thing, I threw it in the bloody hedge."

He was never invited back and the local cats still hang around that same hedge presumably waiting for more flying chub.

I love fly fishing for coarse species and have had great fun with chub, carp, and bream with both dry fly and nymph. I caught a sixteen-pound carp on a black nymph using very light tippet and believe me it went as well as any salmon.

Grayling are of course a game fish, which is probably why they have been accepted by most fly fisherman as worthy targets; but while I have yet to see one being thrown into a bramble bush, they are not to everyone's taste.

In October of 2001 I was approached by the Environment Agency, who had been asked to electro-fish some grayling from one particular beat on the River Test and release them somewhere else. Rules have now changed with regard to fish movement, but at the time the only stipulation was that fish could only be moved within the same river system. If the grayling couldn't be transplanted into another part of the Test, then they would have quite probably been buried in the middle of a field somewhere.

A few days later, the EA turned up with a tank full of grayling to distribute around my beat. I felt as if I was doing these fish a great service by allowing them to be put into the river at Nursling and fully expected immediate induction into the GAS (Grayling Appreciation Society).

The weather was dreadful with constant rain on the day they arrived, and subsequently the banks were very soft and impossible to drive on. I suggested to the EA that they park on the top of the road bridge and fire the fish into the Conegar Pool. It's a beautiful piece of water, about a hundred feet long and fifty feet wide with a depth in the middle of some twelve feet. It tails out at the bottom with some glorious gravely shallows which form a basin around the pool. From July onwards it becomes an amphitheatre of great seatrout up to ten pounds and above. Whilst I was slightly worried about displacing the seatrout when they returned the following season (by October they have all moved on to their spawning grounds)

I didn't think that a few grayling saved from a hole in the ground would do much harm.

I was standing like an expectant father next to the truck when the EA fellows opened the valve on the tank and the grayling began sluicing into the Conegar Pool. At first they came out in ones and twos, grayling of all sizes from a few ounces to several pounds. Then they began to come out in sixes and sevens and a few dozen at a time, then like great flights of teal, and finally like massive undulating flocks of starling. When they finally closed the valve the level in the Conegar had risen by four inches. All told there must have been about two thousand grayling released, and I began to see why these guys from the EA had been so keen to find a watery home for them; it would have taken all day to dig a hole big enough. The Conegar Pool had by now become a boiling whirlpool of mightily impressive dorsal fins and I couldn't help but fear for next year's seatrout migrants.

The EA made a hasty retreat, thanking me for providing a home, and drove off into the sunset leaving me staring into the pool as if it were a cot full of unexpected quintuplets.

Over the next few days I deliberately tried to give the Conegar Pool a wide berth, being somewhat afraid to look into a filthy stew pond full of writhing dorsal fins. Yet when I eventually succumbed and slowly peered over the fringe into the still crystal clear water, I was a bit surprised at what I saw. Massed ranks of calm grayling were meticulously arranged throughout the pool. The gravel shallows were neatly lined with them as if they'd been carefully and very deliberately placed, and great rows of them lay through the arc of the basin as it fell away into the deeper water. They lined the entire pool from end to end and side to side, five or six deep in some places, and in immaculately straight columns.

The Conegar pool, usually home to a few dozen dace and migrating seatrout during the summer months had been invaded by a foreign army which had covertly parachuted from the back of an old EA Land Rover.

The salmon season finishes at Nursling on the last day of September and the river is then let to a couple of different syndicates. A group of coarse fishermen get the bulk of the beat, and the very top portion of the Little River is let to the occasional grayling fisherman (fly only).

A few days after the great grayling liberation, a couple of members of the GAS turned up to fish at Nursling for the first time. They were resplendent in their tweed jackets and beautiful split cane rods with the obligatory wicker basket holding sandwiches with the crusts cut off and flasks of herbal tea. These sorts are plentiful on the chalkstreams and are usually very charming people. Their enjoyment comes as much from the purchasing of unnecessary antique equipment and clothing as in the actual capture of fish.

These two old gentlemen made themselves at home in the fishing lodge, politely turning down my offer of tea because it wasn't called "Earl something or other." They looked at all the pictures and went through all the old fishing records while immersing themselves in the history of Nursling, which was quite obviously what they were most interested in.

On the walls I have some copied pages from the fishing records of the Nursling salmon catches from the 1920's and 30's, which was probably about the period in which these two gentlemen would have rather been fishing. They certainly resembled the photographs we have of people from that era, with handlebar moustaches and old-fashioned clothing, and I suspect that they were also covered in the same thin layer of dust as the pictures.

As everybody does, they lamented the passing of those great days of incredible salmon catches and proceeded to deride the current state of the chalkstreams: no insect life, poor water quality, no fish etc. At a point, I tend to get tired of all this moaning and groaning. While there is little doubt in the overall decline in our rivers, there is also little reason in continually pointing it out.

After sitting for half an hour and reflecting on how great everything was seventy years ago, they began to tackle up and asked if I could give them a quick tour of the beat and to show them any likely grayling spots.

We walked from the lodge around to the Drawing Room Pool, immediately downstream of the now grayling-infested Conegar Pool. We stopped to admire the view across the water meadows and the sight of the Little River meandering towards Southampton waters. I commented that the view had probably not changed that much, although the pylons and high-rise flats of the city in the far distance didn't exactly make for an idyllic oil painting. I told them that I felt the water quality is as good now as it's ever been, and although salmon catches don't measure up to the past, they are slowly improving. They nodded sympathetically and I knew that there was nothing I could say to impress them on the current state of the rivers in comparison to what they deemed the hallowed era of times past.

When they asked again to see the grayling habitat, I decided to draw the noose a bit tighter. "Now *there* is a fish that has flourished under modern conditions and the one fish that is the best indicator of water quality. We've got a good head of them here at Nursling, and if I were you I'd start here and work your way upstream. Have a good look in the next pool up, it's normally a favourite place for grayling."

One of them smiled with a sympathetic and patronizing nod. They then started to fish in the Drawing Room Pool and I went off to hide and watch.

After a bit, one of them slowly wandered towards the Conegar Pool and came to an abrupt halt as he got within about fifteen feet of it. He then sank to his knees and ever so slowly eased his way along the bank, hiding behind the last of the standing fringe. He peered over the fringe into the grayling-infested water and immediately ducked down again, rolling onto his back and laying motionless in the wet grass trying to gather his thoughts. You could see his mind racing through the pictures that his eyes were sending, yet he wasn't feeling confident enough to crawl over to his fishing mate and tell him that the next pool was full of thousands of those things that are dependant on the purest of water.

He eventually climbed back onto his knees and shuffled the

length of the pool with his hands shading his eyes from the midday sun. He must have spent twenty minutes crawling up and down the pool, standing behind trees, shaking his head and rubbing his eyes.

He eventually crept away from the pool and casually wandered towards his friend who was still fishing down below. He stood alongside him for a few minutes, obviously trying to think of the right words, and then he began to gesture towards the Conegar Pool.

As the pair of them reached the pool, the first one sank to his knees and with a small giggle he told his mate to do likewise. Together, these tweed-clad friends began to crawl toward the water's edge on hands and knees. They slowly rose to their feet, and for the next several minutes they walked up and down the pool shaking their heads and pointing out the biggest fish. Occasionally they'd shake hands, but not once did they cast.

With some unfinished work requiring my time, I snuck away from my hide and left them on the banks of the Conegar.

I didn't see them when they left at the end of the day, nor have I heard from them since. Their only trace was a short entry that was made into the fishing book: "Thank you Donny, lovely day at beautiful Nursling. Water quality excellent!"

Over the next few weeks the weather worsened and the river took on its typical winter colour. By the next spring the Conegar Pool was back to normal with nary a grayling to be seen. Where they went, I don't know—maybe they thumbed a ride over to the Itchen?

A Twenty-Pound Nursling Salmon

t is always exciting to catch an Atlantic salmon, no matter what size, but I still feel strangely ashamed to admit that the excitement increases with the size of the fish. "Perfectly natural," I hear the game fisherman shout. "Just a typical man thing," every wife in the land replies.

My biggest salmon at Nursling is a twenty-pounder that I caught in August of 2002. And while not as financially rewarding as the first monster caught by my young mates and me, this one started with Vic, which made it just as memorable.

One day he casually mentioned that he'd noticed a rather large fish holding in Paul's Breakwater. "It be either a big salmon or small dolphin, one or t'other," Vic said.

Bearing in mind that Vic has caught a forty-pound salmon at Nursling, and many in the high thirties, I was in a rush to get a glimpse of this fish, so I followed him up to the breakwater.

Vic slowed up and spoke quietly as we got near to where the fish was and pointed down into the crystal clear water, "There 'tis, nice fishy, looks 'bout eighteen to twenty."

Sure enough the fish was there, almost motionless as if suspended on invisible wires, its massive dorsal giving the slightest wave to hold station and its huge pectorals rippling in the current. Twenty-pound fish on some of the Scottish rivers are two a penny and not an unusual sight, but to see a fish of this size in a crystal clear chalkstream, four feet deep and no more than twelve feet across, seemed to magnify it to goliath proportions. I can't imagine what Vic's forty-pounder might've looked like in this same water.

Over the next few days this fish became something of an attraction, and many Nursling fishermen spent hours either staring at the fish or attempting to catch it. Nobody got close and so it was duly decided that the monster was un-catchable.

On the third day, I was having the usual cup of tea with Vic in the fishing hut and he asked what I was doing in the afternoon as there were no fishermen to look after. I thought he was going to propose a visit to the driving range to slice a few golf balls, but he instead suggested that I go and try to catch the big salmon.

Vic then left for his dinner asking me to phone him once I'd caught the fish. I finished the tea, took my rod off the wall and changed the leader to twenty-pound breaking strain. I tied on a black J.W weighted nymph, put a landing net on my back, and strolled toward our un-catchable fish.

There are times when I fly fish when I feel as if I'm going to catch fish. It's difficult to explain, but it's just a feeling that comes over me for no obvious reason, and it does make me fish with a purpose and confidence. I always like to take advantage of this feeling, as more often than not when fly fishing for salmon on the Test, confidence is not at the top of the list. So there I was, strolling towards an elusive twenty-pounder, Mr. Golden Bollocks Jammy Lucky Bastard. With a feeling of confidence verging on cocksure, I couldn't possibly fail. There's no such thing as an un-catchable fish. Watch this.

I walked with purpose until I reached Paul's Breakwater and then slowed to a creep as I neared the spot where the fish had been holding. With the bankside foliage as a screen, I crawled past his assumed position on my hands and knees until I was about fifteen feet upstream. There, I slowly nestled into the orange balsam, taking extra time in every movement, until I felt safe to slowly lift my head and gauge my quarry's position. The sun was high in the sky and the salmon was very easy to spot with his shadow silhouetted onto the brilliant white gravel beneath him.

The weighted nymphs that we use are very difficult to cast conventionally and I have the scars on the back of my head to prove it. Although I have yet to be shot with an air rifle, I imagine it feels about the same. The only way to cast them with a trout rod is with a roll cast and a very short leader. The whole idea is to slowly bring the nymph up through the salmon's eye-line, perhaps a couple of feet in front of him.

Obviously, making a long and accurate cast with a nymph that weighs almost as much as the rod, while trying to remain out of sight up to your eyeballs in balsam, is not an easy task. As a general rule, salmon are spooky and sensitive fish and too much false casting can put them down when they're holding in clear water. Also, your first shot needs to be on the money as your odds of a take decrease significantly each time he sees your fly. Of course this is not a golden rule, I've seen a fisherman wearing a day-glow green coat entice a salmon while standing nearly astride the fish and casting with the finesse of a twenty stone-ballet dancer.

With the great fish holding very nearly motionless in the current, I pulled off about ten feet of line onto the path and then cast it out into the river about fifteen feet upstream of him. With that, I pulled off another ten feet of line and lifted the nymph to the top, roll cast it out again, and then immediately rolled another loop of line directly upstream of that. As the nymph drifted towards the salmon, the slack was taken out of the loop of line lying on the water. I stopped the rod and the nymph slowly lifted from the bottom up towards the surface. With one quick flick of its tail the salmon was behind it, drawn by either aggression or annoyance. I remember seeing that wonderful white throat as the fish took the nymph and turned downwards, his tail folding over on top of the water as he returned to his lay.

Not realizing how close I had crept to the river, when I stood and lifted into the fish I lost my footing and slid down the bank. If I'd been quick enough to take the landing net off of my back, I could have not only hooked a twenty-pounder, but also landed it all within about three seconds. Luckily I managed to stop before landing on top of the salmon, and as I inched my way back up the bank I glanced around to make sure no one had witnessed yet another of my slightly unprofessional moments.

The salmon had returned to its original position, and when I regained my composure I found him sitting there as if nothing had happened. Did he even know he was hooked? I put as much pressure on him as I dared, and my rod arched into an impossibly deep bend with the line singing a tune. The salmon didn't move and a kind of uneasy standoff began. That's when I phoned Vic.

"Ello Donny, you caught 'im 'aven't you?" I was halfway through telling him where I was when he said, "On me way Donny, well done me boy."

Within five minutes Vic was hurrying up the bank to the spot where I stood tight to the salmon. The fish was still glued to the bottom of the river, and after quickly assessing the situation Vic announced, like an airport tannoy, that we'd land him in forty-five minutes at approximately five hundred feet downstream in the Conegar Pool. He then suggested that I needed to give the fish a bit more pressure, otherwise we'd be late.

The next twenty minutes consisted mainly of me wading downstream behind the fish and trying not to let him have too much line. Every few minutes the fish would give a quick flick of its tail and surge upstream, and then slowly turn and head back down. On several such circuits he passed nearly close enough for me to touch, but he wasn't ready for the net. Where we were, the waterline was about ten feet below the steep banks and that's where Vic was standing, shadowing the fight, and giving out helpful advice like "You forgot to put waders on, Donny. Must be bloody wet, and cold."

As we made our way downstream, the road bridge began to get my attention. The river went under the lane through two small stone arches with a clearance of only two feet. This, I thought, could be a problem, although I was confident that Vic would have a cunning plan. When we arrived just upstream of the road bridge, the fish tucked himself up under the far bank and my daughter Jodie, who was playing in our garden opposite, asked me what I was doing in the river with no waders on.

I explained that I was just taking a salmon for a walk and could she please go and get her Mum and tell her to bring the video camera.

The fish eventually turned downstream and went through the bridge accompanied by gasps of amazement as the kids, who were stood on the bridge, saw it at close hand for the first time. So there I stood, up to my gonads in icy water, with my salmon fifty feet below me in the Conegar pool and the road bridge separating us. My silent contemplation was interrupted by Vic who was stood on the road bridge talking to my wife, "Go into the rod room and get the gaff, my dear, 'tis 'anging on the wall and we'll soon 'ave the bugger out."

Vic has used the gaff hundreds of times before, but in this day and age of catch and release he planned to use it in a different way. His idea was to use the hook to carefully pick up the line downstream of the bridge, but after ten minutes of trying he admitted defeat.

"Give 'er a try, Donny, me eyes ain't what they were."

From my spot in the river above the bridge, I passed the rod up to Vic and climbed out onto the bank, and then to the bridge. I took the gaff, and after a couple of attempts, picked up the line from the downstream side. I now had the fly line in my hand with a twenty-pound salmon on the other end. Just as I began to ask Vic what to do next he shouted out, "I've thrown the rod in Donny, you should see it any time now." So not only was I playing a salmon with one hand, I was now frantically using my other hand to gather the slack fly line that was attached to my £500 fly rod. It was probably the most expensive game of Poohsticks that I've ever been involved in.

As the tip of my fly rod came through the bridge, I transferred the line to my mouth and frantically gathered up the slack. After lifting the rod from the water and reeling up the remaining slack, I once again passed the rod to Vic and climbed down off the bridge to the bank of the Conegar Pool. When Vic handed back the rod I found myself on level ground with a tight line and a salmon still firmly attached, and occasionally jumping.

On the bank opposite the Conegar Pool is a private house with a garden that comes right to the water's edge. There were eight or nine ladies having a coffee in the garden and they looked on in astonishment as we all came into view. Once the ladies realised what was happening, they joined our troupe, and stood watching the drama unfold while drinking their coffee, laced with gin, I'm sure.

I felt a lot more confident about actually landing the fish once we were in the Conegar Pool, mainly because that's where Vic said we were going to land it, which, according to my watch, would be in another six and a half minutes. The fish was still cruising around the pool in deep water, although occasionally I could pull him almost to the top. He was beginning to tire and Vic pulled the landing net off my back. After one or two near misses I got him to the top again and slowly eased him toward the net. Vic carefully slid the net under the great fish and gently lifted him from the Test. Once on the bank he looked massive and I quickly took the nymph out and held the fish up for a photograph.

The looks of amazement on the kids' faces were fantastic, and the "oohs" and "aahs" from the ladies opposite was the perfect background accompaniment. I was indeed a mighty game fisher-man and this was my moment of glory. Never before, nor since, have I held something so proudly in my hands and got such a reac-tion from a group of ladies. They all stood and politely applauded as Vic and I took a bow. The fish was back in the water within fif-teen seconds and after a minute of holding him, swam off into the pool. I stood up, shook Vic by the hand and we both posed for the camera. It is the most amazing piece of video footage that I'll ever have and I'll treasure it always, me and my kids, a twenty-pound smoothie and the legendary Vic Foot.

I was on cloud nine as we walked towards the fishing hut to toast our latest capture. I had joined the Twenty-Pound Nursling Salmon Club and thought that perhaps even Vic was impressed. I took two coffee mugs from the cupboard and poured about half a pint of whisky into each one. I raised my mug to Vic and the salmon and felt that wonderful feeling of comradeship and belonging, and just as I was about to get carried away, Vic raised his whisky and said, "Well done Donny, that were a lovely fish. Mine you, good job it weren't a biggun t'other wise we'd never got the bastard out!"

A Bottle of £2 Vintage

'll be completely honest, here: if I close my eyes and take a sip from a glass of wine, regardless of its price or vintage, I cannot tell you whether it's red or white. Does that seem odd? Well, I also drink Guinness from a can, my favourite lunch is a cheese and Marmite sandwich, and I like the pickled onion flavoured Monster Munch. A connoisseur of fine taste I am not, although I know what I like and I like what I know.

I've never been keen on someone telling me what I should or shouldn't buy because of fashion, perception, or pricing. Whether it's food, wine, art, or clothing, why should I listen to some young toffee-nosed twat from London who fancies himself an authority on what I like to eat, drink, wear, or look at? Just because he wears the title of "critic" doesn't make him an expert. My grandfather smoked for much of his ninety-two year span. Did he consider himself an expert on tobacco? No—but had he offered advice on that matter, I'd have darn sure listened.

With all of the anal banter and comparison about gear, clothing, and chic fishing destinations these days, it irks me that the completely pointless knowledge of wine has also found its way into fishing lodge dinner conversations.

If you ever come to Nursling as a guest, you'd better believe that a return invitation will be wholly dependant on the supposed quality of wine that you bring on that first visit. And, fellow, if that bottle costs less than your fly rod, then you'd better have a bloody good explanation.

I'm kidding, of course, but oftentimes the wine discussions at Nursling do lend that air of snobbery.

Yes, Rupert's guest seems to be a nice chap, and casts a good line, but I couldn't help but notice that dreadful 1996 Chardonnay in his basket. Terrible year; you can buy it in Cherbourg for about four quid. Don't think we'll be seeing him again.

Surprisingly, I do drink quite a lot of wine in the fishing lodge, but only to be sociable and because I'd be rude to refuse. I've often thought that's probably the typical opening line used at most Alcoholics Anonymous meetings. *No, I haven't got a drink problem, my Mum always told me to be polite and outgoing.*

I just can't understand all of the fuss that surrounds wine. I've never once wondered where a pint of Guinness originated or in which year it was brewed. It tastes good, that's all I care about. To me, wine tastes disgusting, and occasionally it tastes just awful. My palate is not suited to fine wine, nor am I inclined to bluff my way through it by pretentiously extolling the virtues of a southern facing vineyard in the North of Italy. Give me a can of the black stuff and I'll be fine—or even better, something made from grain.

I'm often intrigued by the relationship of host and guest around the dinner table at Nursling. It typically starts with the host politely asking the guest about previous fishing trips and which ghillie he has fished with on a certain Scottish river. When the fishing scrutiny ends, the guest might offer a joke or a funny story, but never his best one because he wouldn't want to steal the thunder from the host.

From there the subject typically turns to wine, whereby a serious silence will befall the room as the guest unveils his offering. I normally feel sorry for the guest, because the curiosity and scrutiny is so absurd that he may as well be flopping his dick onto the table.

The next few seconds can make or break a fishing guest while the regulars sit back, nod, and silently contemplate the merits, origin, and vintage of the offering (the wine, not his dick).

After putting up with all this posturing and pageantry for many seasons, I decided that I'd have a bit of fun with a group of wine connoisseurs that fished Nursling in 2002. There were seven rods in the group, six regulars and one guest, and each of them had brought a couple of bottles of wine. Of course, the discussion of each bottle soon turned into a heated debate about where it was from, the relative humidity of that region, and what size feet are best for pressing the bloody grapes.

With each glass consumed the rods became more pissed and opinionated, and by dinnertime they began emphatically arguing the merits of their own offerings while criticising the bottles of their rivals. I decided to spring my prank into action when one of the fishermen suggested that he had seen more life in his spaniel's scrotum than was in a glass of his friend's treasured Chardonnay.

In the kitchen of the fishing lodge I found two or three bottles of their red wine already opened, so I went over to the house and fetched a bottle of Mrs. Wickham's Blackberry & Nettle wine from the cupboard beneath the stairs. Mrs. Wickham was the local magistrate and we had generously purchased her potion (for two quid) from the school fair about ten years prior. She was known for her attempts to make alcohol from anything close at hand, and even with my amateur palate I realised after one sniff that this stuff could quite easily run an outboard motor.

I took the Wickham's back over to the fishing lodge and sneaked it past the experts, who were loudly discussing the advantages offered by Portuguese cork. In the kitchen I poured the contents of one of their more expensive wines into a saucepan and carefully refilled the bottle with the Blackberry & Nettle. I then transferred the wine in the saucepan back into Mrs. Wickham's bottle with the £2 price tag and the label proudly proclaiming, "It'll put hair on your chest!"

When the switch was complete, I put both bottles back on the kitchen table and made my way back to the dining room. As I sat alongside the still debating fishermen thinking what a clever, scheming bastard I was, the more vociferous of the wine experts rose to his feet and asked who would like another glass. It occurred to me when he left the room that perhaps my prank was a bad idea, but at that point there was no turning back.

As the expert entered the kitchen to inspect the offerings, the guest rod, Charles, called out for him to bring in the 1989 bottle of something-or-other that he had proudly brought to share with the group. Charles was a lovely man who was thrilled at the invitation to fish at Nursling, and I squirmed in my chair thinking that my experiment might cause him terrible embarrassment.

I was still thinking of admitting my prank when I heard the expert yell from the kitchen, "What the hell is this? Mrs. Wickham's what? Two bloody quid!"

The expert had found the Blackberry & Nettle bottle, the one that actually contained the prized 1989 something-or-other that Charles, the guest, had brought. "Hope this isn't your offering Charles," the expert bellowed, "Two bloody quid, whose is this crap?"

The expert was now beginning to get up my nose and without any thought about the inevitable consequences, a gremlin within forced me to say, "Actually it's mine. Mrs. Wickham is a friend of my Mum and I thought I'd amuse you wine experts with a bottle of her plonk."

The challenge was on.

The expert walked in with the Wickham's bottle, poured a little into his glass, sarcastically held it up to the light, and then wafted the expensive wine under his nose.

"Bloody well hope it tastes better than it looks," he snarled as he continued to gaze into the glass. He then raised the glass to his lips, sipped at the wine, and like a master comedian playing to his captivated audience, he contorted his face as if drinking vinegar before the finale of spraying the wine back into his glass and staggering backwards as if he'd been shot.

"God help us," he gasped, "that Wickham is trying to poison us!"

His audience fell about laughing, but feeling obliged to join in the criticism they cautiously poured a little into their own glasses

Most followed the routine of disgust although one or two said that it wasn't that bad. When one of the rods said that he actually liked it, the others howled with laughter and ridicule. With a strange look that made me feel slightly uncomfortable, Charles didn't pass comment after tasting the wine, but sat carefully examining the bottle and quietly reading the label.

After phase one of the prank was complete, the expert rose from table and went to the kitchen to fetch the 1989 something-or-other bottle, which of course contained the £2 Blackberry & Nettle. "Now then," announced the expert, "Let's have a proper wine. Where did you get this one from Charles?"

After removing the cork, he went through the same routine of holding it up to the light and waving it beneath his nose. From across the room, even I could tell that it looked more like pale ale than wine, and I could also see that the expert was quite confused. Again, he held the wine aloft to more closely examine its colour, and then he gingerly took another sniff, this time with the glass a bit further from his nose. There was no repeat of the facial contortions when he sipped very delicately from the glass, but I did detect an involuntary shudder, followed by a very deliberate gulping swallow, a long exhale, and a glazed expression.

"Well," he said with a squeaky nasal pitch and a single teardrop wandering down his cheek, "It's certainly different, and has a very distinctive flavouring. I like it, thank you Charles, you can come again…probably."

After the others poured a sip and sampled the vile brew, there were a variety of reviews with some saying it was "pleasant," others that it was "alright" and a couple of honest ones saying they wouldn't have given it to their pet guinea pigs. While I was chuckling internally at the expert's buffoonery, I was still concerned about the complete lack of response from Charles. He most definitely knew what was going on and sat silently at the table trying to work out who was attempting to discredit him.

I was in a quandary as to what my next move should be as most of the fishermen had quite happily gone along with the expert's ridiculous opinion of the two wines and I feared they would not find an admission on my part to be very funny. I had made them look foolish but it was only me, and possibly Charles, who knew it. To have admitted everything would have well and truly set the cat amongst the pigeons. When they moved on to another bottle (one not tampered with) I decided that silence was the best option and the drinking went on without another word about the prank.

When the group began gathering their things to leave, Charles thanked me for a lovely day, gave me a splendid tip, and as he walked to the door he turned and said, "Give my regards to Mrs. Wickham and tell her to charge more for her wine. You can't possibly have a bottle of vintage for two quid, even if it's made from nettles."

I smiled, and there and then decided that Charles would definitely be coming again to Nursling, even if I had to be the one to invite him.

Stop The River, I Want To Get Off

fter a few years of working alongside a river, it became
apparent that the general public is largely ignorant to the
life of a chalkstream, or, for that matter any type of flowing water.
Most people aren't particularly interested in the science or the technical details of how a river works, but as I have learned, many don't
even realise that a river usually runs downhill.

Unfortunately, it's not just the unknowing public that seems
lost on a river's true form and function; the people who set themselves up as our environmental saviours are often just as blind.
These oligarchic self-appointed men of the committees seem to be
in a perpetual state of low civil unrest. One faction can't agree with
the other and their squabbling and bickering carries on while the
river slowly and methodically runs past them towards the sea.

During my work as a riverkeeper, I am constantly reminded
of this alarming ignorance and failing within "the management,"
although I always try to point out the bleeding obvious to both
amateur and professional in an equally un-patronising way.

This sometimes leads to drink.

During the hopefully glorious late spring and early summer days of June and July, the river and surrounding catchment area becomes a phenomenal growing machine. The ranunculus grows as quickly as you can cut it, as do the pathways, willow trees, and fringe alongside the river. This is a busy time for any chalkstream keeper. All of this trimming and pollarding, together with stocking duties and looking after the fishermen, means for early mornings and late nights.

Of course, cutting the weed and grass on a regular basis only encourages it to grow again, and indeed that is half the purpose of such management. Yet, as rewarding as it all may look, I guarantee that there is not a riverkeeper on any chalkstream in England who has at one time in his life not wished for that magic on/off switch to buy a moment's rest.

Mother Nature has quite rightly not cared that the busiest time for the riverkeeper also coincides with the busiest time for the fisherman, and the two don't mix well. Having somebody cutting a few tons of ribbon weed upstream of you does not make for great fishing, nor does being nearly run over by a three-ton mower driven by an over-worked keeper trying to finish his five miles of pathways. To keep the river looking exactly the same each time you turn up for your once a month visit takes hours of hard work, and during this busiest of times it has to be completed before fishermen arrive or after they have buggered off home.

Sorry, after they have *gone* home.

Over the years, a few infamous keepers have tried to halt this never-ending workload and buy themselves a somewhat easier life. The scorched earth policy has been used on a few chalkstream beats, although thankfully it's rarely used today.

An old keeper on a neighbouring beat told me years ago about a very large willow tree that had become a bane to the underkeepers whose job it was to sweep the seemingly endless supply of falling leaves off the paths. "Soon as I got the head keeper's job, first thing I did was chop the sodding thing down! No more bloody leaves," he said with a *what a clever bastard I am* look on his face.

I glanced down at his feet and studied his boots for a second. "What you looking at?" he asked.

"Well I was wondering whether or not you've applied the same thought process with your feet and no longer have to cut your toenails?"

Many trees have been felled, fringes pulled up, and pathways covered, all in the false hope of an easier life—but ultimately at the expense of a healthy river. It's a hard fact of nature that seemingly pointless things that require annoying maintenance will always grow on both the riverbanks and our persons.

Fishermen are also pretty good at questioning the blindingly obvious and some of their helpful observations are at times difficult to comprehend. I remember walking up the river one day during a fantastic mayfly hatch and seeing a fisherman rooted to the spot holding his rod out at right angles to the river with his fly sat (and dragging) on the surface under the tip. When I got around to where he was, I questioned him on his rather unusual dry fly technique.

"Casting is a rather important part of the equation," I told him, "Why are you dangling your fly in one spot?"

He looked completely unfazed as he replied, "Well I have been doing what you said and casting upstream, but the bloody fly keeps coming back downstream towards me and I have to do it again!"

On another occasion, an experienced angler who had fished at Nursling for many years asked if I'd mind him giving me a bit of advice. Having taken the job only a few months earlier, I readily accepted and told him that I wanted the Nursling anglers to feel they had a voice. We sat down in the fishing lodge and I edged a little closer in anticipation of receiving a brilliant suggestion which this wise old rod had gleaned from many years of fishing the Test.

"Donny old boy," he said with a grandfatherly look in his eye, "There's a big rock in the middle of the Little River just below the Stone Breakwater—in fact I believe that's why it's *called* the Stone Breakwater. Anyway, there is almost always a salmon laid in front of that rock, which seems to be a fantastic place for them. The trouble is that you have to fish that spot from downstream and, try as I may, I can't keep from hooking that bloody rock. Perhaps, Donny, if you could move the rock out of the way, we'd have a better chance of catching the salmon."

I'm still not entirely sure that he wasn't taking the piss, but needless to say my confidence in taking advice from fishermen, no matter how experienced, took something of a decisive blow. Anyhow I thought I'd humour him.

"Yes, you're right," I told him, "It is amazing how often you see a rock behind a salmon or indeed a breakwater in front of one, an incredible coincidence. Of course it could be that the two are somehow connected, but I expect it is just happenstance. Then again, and I'm probably sounding a little naïve here, it could be that the reason the salmon lies there is because of the rock and if you were to take the rock away then maybe the salmon would bugger off."

He pondered my inexperienced suggestion for a while before eventually shaking his head and saying, "No, no, the salmon probably likes that particular spot for a variety of reasons, although I do agree that it is strange how often you do see a rock behind a salmon."

Needless to say, after one or two months of listening to expert advice, I began to go with my gut feelings. Fishermen fish the river and keepers keep it, best to leave it at that.

Perhaps the most glaring example of misunderstanding of the workings of a river came from a different source, thankfully neither keeper or fisherman. The Nursling Mill sits astride the river alongside the main hatches that control the levels of the Test for miles upstream. During winter flooding all ten of the main hatches are fully open and the big mill hatch is also wound up giving maximum relief to the river.

As you can imagine, the amount of water during these floods is phenomenal and the power of the flow is menacing. Once the floods subside, the hatch in the mill is the first to be closed and during low water years may remain shut for the full twelve months. That closure stems the main flow although there is always a nominal amount going through just to keep the millrace running clear. The Nursling Mill was built in 1728 but hasn't been used since the

1950's. The internal machinery is still in place, though I doubt it's fully operable.

At about the time I started at Nursling, the mill was turned into three very posh apartments that are let out on a monthly basis with a fair turnover of tenants living the dream of life in a Hampshire water mill. Some stay for quite a while, and some are only there for a couple of months before the rather hefty rental bites into that dream and they move on, ambition fulfilled.

As I have access to the mill because of the need to operate the internal hatch, I get to meet all the new tenants and enjoy showing them the history and the workings of the mill. Over the years I have become something of a tourist guide with a real fascination and intrigue about the place and the people who have worked there over the centuries.

One particular couple moved into the main apartment in February 2003 and showed a keen interest in both the history and especially in how a water mill actually worked. I can remember being a little surprised in their apparent worry at the proximity of the water. "It seems a bit dangerous this close to the river," the wife remarked.

I wasn't entirely sure that they weren't pulling my leg, as I always think that being called a "water mill" probably gives enough clues as to its general whereabouts.

After they'd been there about three weeks I received a phone call from the mill's landlord, who told me that there was a problem with the new tenants and he would bring over a copy of a letter of complaint that also involved me. It was a confusing conversation, because while it sounded a little worrying and I racked my brain to think how I could possibly have upset them, the landlord was either giggling, or perhaps sobbing, throughout the entire call.

He did indeed arrive the next day with a copy of the aforementioned letter that he pressed into my hand, telling me not to worry too much.

I sat down to read the letter with a nervous feeling in the pit of my stomach, still trying to think how I'd upset these seemingly charming people. The letter was beautifully hand-written in a very professional manner and at first stated how pleased they were with the general condition of their apartment and what a great place it was to live. It went on to say how helpful the riverkeeper had been and how I had even offered to teach them how to cast a fly rod. I read on with ever increasing confusion until I got to the last couple of lines, and I roughly quote. "There is only one area where we could see some improvement to us living in such an idyllic place and that is in the noise that the river makes. You can at times hear it whilst lying in bed at night. Would it be possible to ask the riverkeeper to stop the river at night-time so as to ensure a good night's sleep? We understand that the mill is no longer worked so we presume the water can be stopped at any time. I would politely request that the best time for us would be between 7pm and 8am, and perhaps the occasional weekend—and certainly bank holidays when friends visit."

This is why most riverkeepers tend to be fairly heavy drinkers, smoke when they don't really want to, and eventually lose all faith in mankind.

Stop the bloody river indeed.

The Golden Roller

t was about the beginning of April 2003, and the horizontal
drizzle swept by a chilly northeasterly meant that the river was
not in great order. I was sat in the fishing lodge waiting for my rods
to arrive and wondering how disappointed they'd be at the state of
the Little River and the lack of fish. We hadn't even seen a bloody
kelt in recent days, much less a fresh run springer.

I glanced at my watch with frustration as I remembered the
last words from the annoying twit who had bought the day and
then sold it on for a twenty-percent markup.

"For God's sake, make sure that you're not late," he demand-
ed, "They're very important people and not used to waiting."

I've never been late for anyone and didn't appreciate him
suggesting so, but I was sat in the lodge well before time and again
looked at my watch. My "very important" people were now forty
minutes late, themselves, and I was thinking of phoning the twit to
ask why the on time arrangement didn't appear to work both ways.

As it was, I heard a car pull up on the road outside the fishing
lodge and peered out of the window as the doors opened. It was a
black London cab and the driver still had that smug *I've just made*

a hundred and fifty quid grin on his face as he pulled a couple of large leather bags out of the back.

The passenger pulled out a great wad of notes that looked to be about three million quid, peeled off a few, and handed them to the cabbie. The smug grin quickly disappeared when the cabbie realised he could have doubled the fare without the passenger actually giving a damn.

The passenger caught sight of me looking from the window and gave a smile and a wave. The taxi driver was then dismissed and I went out to greet the guest and help him into the lodge with his two leather suitcases. He introduced himself, explaining that he was the host for the day and had two people coming to fish, both of which were very keen anglers. He said they had some very important business to discuss and they thought that a chalkstream was as good a place as any.

This man had an incredible presence and intrigue about him, and my cautious admiration quickly turned to undying love when he pressed a week's wages into my hand, and again emphasised, "very important."

This was to be the first, and sadly only time, that I would meet Stephen Curtis, the immensely successful London attorney. As we sat in the lodge drinking coffee he said that his two guests would arrive shortly after eleven and he had already instructed their chauffer to drive into the paddock and park alongside the fishing lodge.

Right on cue we sensed their car approaching and my coffee cup hovered in front of my open mouth as I stared out the window at the magnificent gold Rolls Royce gliding silently toward the lodge.

The immaculately dressed chauffer seemed to float around the car as he opened the passenger door with a smooth professional elegance. I wouldn't have been totally surprised to see Snow White step from the car, such was the fairytale atmosphere, and I immediately wished that I had cut the grass in the paddock before they arrived.

An old pair of leather boots was the first thing to emerge from the car, closely followed by a tatty pair of Levis and an unshaven young man who would have looked more at home rounding up cattle on the plains of Montana. He even had a rolled up cigarette hanging from the corner of his mouth.

The chauffer floated to the other side of the car and another cowboy got out stretching and yawning as if he'd been asleep in a stagecoach. While Stephen greeted his friends and introduced them to me, the second cowboy produced a pouch of tobacco and rolled up a smoke of his own. I'm not often fazed by the prestige of my rods, but I knew that I was in the presence of wealthy and powerful people.

It turned out that the two cowboys were the sons of one of the richest men in Europe and heirs to a massive fortune. They were also fanatical fly fishermen and it was apparent that I was to be a fairly important cog in the day's mix of fishing and worldly business transactions.

I do love my work.

I already had three rods set up and the two cowboys eyed them confidently as we walked down to the river. Stephen also picked one up and followed us down to the waters edge, although he said that he'd just watch us for a while and get ready with the landing net.

After a few minutes of demonstration, I noticed a decent fish move from in front of one of the stones in the pool and told one of the cowboys to fish over it. The water was a bit coloured and I couldn't make out the species, but when the cowboy hooked up I could tell by the lazy fight that it wasn't a springer.

While his friend fought the fish, Stephen stood alongside and offered an excited commentary, "It's a salmon, Donny, isn't it? It's a beautiful salmon, look at the bloody size of it!"

It was actually a seatrout kelt of about six pounds, but such was Stephen's excitement and want for a great fish, that it indeed remarkably became one. Remembering that hefty wad of notes in Stephen's pocket, I replied, "Yes a lovely fish, looks about twelve pounds. Well done, a great bit of fishing."

After only a couple of minutes, the poor old seatrout gave up the fight and came in like a carrier bag. "Christ these springers fight well!" Stephen exclaimed, "Look at the size of it!"

He was almost delirious with excitement and had the camera working overtime. I did my best to avoid being snapped with this "beauty" because my reputation would have been in tatters had my contemporaries seen me posing with a spawned-out seatrout. Fearing that someone might be spying from the hedges, I released the kelt as quickly as I could and breathed a sigh of relief as it drifted back into the Drawing Room Pool to resume its sleep.

Stephen and his two guests were still shaking hands and congratulating each other. I think they probably all knew that the fish was an old kelt, but everyone maintained the charade for fear of hurting someone's feelings and jeopardizing the impending business transaction. After all the backslapping, Stephen insisted that he was going to stay behind and that the two cowboys and I should go on downstream to find some more of these silver torpedoes that were quite obviously piling into the Little River on each new tide.

As we began to make our way downstream, Stephen walked back towards the fishing lodge to assist the chauffer with the boxes that he had removed from the Rolls. There was a sizeable stack; some big, some small, and some wrapped in fancy paper. Perhaps we were going to play party games as well?

As we wandered off down river, the cowboys again produced their smoking paraphernalia, but this time they began rolling up cigarettes of greater potency. Several years spent in Alabama didn't teach me too much about life, but recognising different kinds of marijuana became a speciality of mine. This was a good strain, expensive too. Of course, when they invited me to partake I felt obligated to do so; it would have been rude not to.

By the time we got down to the lower river, it was obvious that the focus of the day had changed. We were stupidly stoned, so we sat for a while by the Sea Pool Bridge, and laughed at everything that moved while killing time before the planned dinnertime business discussions. The fishing wasn't great, but the swaying balsam was hilarious.

We eventually began to meander our way back upstream, having a few casts as we walked and catching a few trout and the occasional chub. When we got back to the Drawing Room Pool I looked over towards the lodge and saw Stephen asleep on the bench outside. The chauffer-chef turned from tending his fire and gave Stephen a nudge that made him jump to attention and grab his rod as if to suggest he'd been fishing hard all morning. It was one of those moments where I recognise the absurdity of trying to mix business with pleasure. Stephen had spent the morning snoozing on the seat and his clients had spent theirs giggling at the shrubbery.

Walking into the lodge was like being transported back in time to the Victorian splendour of aristocratic life in a top London hotel. The lodge had been transformed into a resplendent dining room with fine cloths, cutlery, and china. The chauffer-chef had now become our waiter, and poured champagne into crystal glasses that Stephen passed to the two cowboys and then to me. "You have dinner with us Donny, you're very welcome my friend."

Stephen instructed us where to sit and I slipped my napkin out of the silver holder, quaffed the champagne, and studied the Cuban cigar lying alongside the china dinner plates. I began to wonder whether the weed wasn't a little stronger than I had first imagined, and whether I was about to be rudely awoken to the usual dinner of a sandwich and cup of coffee. But when the chauffer-chef-waiter asked me how I would like my king prawns cooked, I realised that I was having one of those special once in a life time riverkeeping moments and urged myself not to get completely pissed on the champagne.

The food was nothing short of miraculous. Adding to its glory was the fact that it was cooked outside on a pile of charcoal in a constant drizzle by a bloke who had earlier called himself "just the driver."

The conversation around the table was like something from a James Bond film and included everything from shooting tigers in

India to matching the five hundred million that the Russians were prepared to put in. The chauffer-chef-waiter and myself were occasionally included in the conversation, when it was politely lowered more to our level, and we talked of the plight of both the salmon and Southampton Football Club in equal measures. After a suitably wondrous desert and a coffee that I'd never heard of, we sat back and puffed on Cubans that may have very well cost more than my best fly rod.

Marmite on toast was never going to be the same again.

The conversation went on for another hour or so before Stephen suddenly got to his feet and announced that they were leaving. It was about 3:00 pm and he thought that they would like to go to a stillwater fishery and catch some monster trout, as these salmon were a tad tricky. "Donny I hate to be rude, but would it be okay if we leave you the mess to clear up?" Stephen asked as he pulled one of the cowboys up from his chair.

"No no, that's fine, I'll quickly wash the plates whilst you pack the rods up."

"Well if it's okay with you we'd rather leave everything. You've been absolutely fantastic Donny, thanks for looking after us so well." Stephen folded another couple of fifty-pound notes into my hand and ushered the cowboys towards the car.

We all shook hands. Stephen said he'd be seeing me on a regular basis as he thought that Nursling, in addition to great fishing, was a fine place to do business.

The golden roller glided out of the paddock as quietly and impressively as it had come in and Stephen's hand waved from the window as it eased through the five bar gate into Mill Lane. As I turned back towards the fishing lodge I saw the great stack of boxes piled against the bin, each of them emblazoned with logos from Selfridges or Harrods. It was an expensive pile of rubbish and even the wrapping looked too good to throw away.

My wife had the time of her life clearing the table, and together we finished off the champagne and the wonderful food, and then packed up our new dinner service, cutlery, and crystal. Finally we folded our new tablecloth, along with the napkins and serviettes, and took them over the road into the fishing cottage.

I was very sad to hear that Stephen Curtis was killed in a helicopter crash a few months after his Nursling visit, but not entirely surprised at rumours suggesting Russian mafia involvement in the accident.

I will probably never find out anything else about Stephen Curtis, but I really do hope that the chauffer-chef-waiter wasn't also his helicopter pilot.

Bridge Over The River Test

ne of my more ambitious duties at Nursling involves the
occasional replacement of a footbridge that has been damaged by flood or weakened by time and the elements. The actual
design and construction isn't that daunting, but getting the materi-
als in place often provides a logistical challenge. I usually buy old
telegraph poles for my bridge supports. They're treated with pitch,
which helps them resist rotting. Unfortunately, they're much too
heavy for me to hoist and carry on my shoulder.

In 2003 I had to replace a bridge down on the Little River,
and I began pondering the notion that the natural power of the river could possibly assist me in getting the telegraph poles from the
paddock behind the fishing hut down to the bridge site. If I could
only get them into the river, the poles could be floated downstream
and into position on the high tide.

Brilliant plan, Donny!

As I continued to mull over the plan, it occurred to me that
perhaps I could just build the entire bridge next to the river and
then float the whole caboodle downstream as a finished package.
This had now turned into something of a major civil engineering

project, and I immediately thought of the renowned Victorian engineer, Isambard Kingdom Brunel.

If only he could see me now!

Of course, had I stopped at the one brilliant plan I would probably have been okay. The second stroke of genius was what actually got me into trouble.

Getting the poles down to the riverbank was easy enough, and the construction of the bridge was a piece of cake. It was a simple design whereby two telegraph poles were laid parallel and four-foot boards nailed across the tops. I doubt the design would have turned many heads among Mr. Brunel's colleagues, but it more than served the purpose. Once the bridge was finished, however, the actual launching process proved trickier than I had thought.

After much blood, sweat, tears, swearing, and some help from my motorized dumper, I was finally able to move the bridge to a point where it teetered atop the pilings adjacent the Drawing Room Pool. The water level was about three feet below the pilings, and the pool itself was about ten feet deep.

As I stood looking at my new bridge balanced above the pool, I began to wonder whether or not it would actually float. I'm sure that all great civil engineers have these nervous moments, but the thought of my bridge being launched into the Drawing Room Pool and sinking like a stone was a sobering one. I can't imagine the designer of the Queen Mary having quite the same worry, but I'll bet he was secretly relieved after she slid down the rails and bobbed on the surface.

With a mix of scepticism and confidence, I gave the bridge a shove and then stood back to admire my personal Queen Mary floating proudly in anticipation of her maiden voyage. After securely mooring her to the bank, I stepped aside and contemplated the impending half-mile journey down the Little River, which I presumed would be the easy bit.

Even though she floated high and proud, it became apparent that steering the thing would be no easy task. Sitting atop my bridge with a length of 2x4 for a steering pole, I shoved away from the bank and began my descent. Using the steering pole to push away from the breakwaters, and lying flat while going under bridges, I negotiated two-thirds of the run without much problem. When I hit the falling tide in the lower river, I had no choice but to pull the bridge up next to the bank, tie it to the fence, and wait for the next day's high tide to complete my journey.

It was raining hard by the time I secured the bridge, and it continued to rain for much of the next three days. The ensuing floods meant a busy time for me working the hatch gates, and I'm sorry to say that I didn't really give the bridge project another thought for the rest of the week.

When the rains stopped and the flooding subsided on the upper beats, I did finally venture down the Little River and was startled to see how much the water had risen. I couldn't actually see the meadow where my bridge was moored, let alone the bridge itself. As I waded toward where it should have been, I had visions of it wiping out a few dozen racing yachts out on the Solent Sea.

Yes, constable, there we were happily sailing along when this bridge made from telegraph poles rammed our starboard side.

Right-o, sir, now just blow into this bag for me please.

As I waded along considering the possible insurance disclaimers, I finally happened upon the missing bridge. I was relieved to see it still in the same meadow, albeit five hundred yards across the other side. As the water receded, my bridge was left resting near the fence running alongside the Test Way walk.

The particular meadow in which my bridge was marooned happened to be leased by the Wildlife Trust for nature viewing and bird watching. I'd once gotten stuck up to my axles in the same meadow in my dumper after they had refused me permission to drive across it. I left the dumper running and went to get a shovel in a futile attempt to dig myself out before being seen, but when I returned the gentle vibration of the running engine had buried it to the point of no return. A twenty-ton excavator wouldn't have dug me out, let alone yours truly and a bloody shovel.

Without a better idea, I climbed back into the seat with the boggy marsh water up to my waist, started the engine, and tried one last time to get the machine unstuck. It didn't work (it never does), and when the engine finally sputtered and succumbed to the flooded bog, I looked up and saw some of the Wildlife Trust people staring at me in disbelief from across the meadow.

With a confident grin, I waved to acknowledge their stares and to let them know, of course, that I was totally in control of the situation. They returned my wave with smug looks that said, *we told you so you total prick of a riverkeeper.* Given the depth to which I buried the dumper, to them I probably appeared to be sat alone in the middle of a marsh holding a steering wheel.

The humiliation of the sunken dumper was still fresh in my mind as I stood staring at my stranded bridge. The marsh was still flooded and I knew that I had to move it quickly before the tide went out and left it high and dry within full view of the Wildlife Trust.

With my adrenaline surging, I quickly pulled the bridge away from the fence, across the footpath, and into the flooded meadow. From there I heaved and shoved it across the marsh and back to the banks of the swollen river. Had I stopped there and regained control of my senses, the outcome would have been much different. Instead, however, I pushed the bridge straight into the muddy flow and hopped aboard.

The Little River was unrecognisable as a small chalkstream and looked more like the Ganges during runoff; but there I was, kneeling on a runaway bridge, hurtling toward the estuary with little thought toward the consequences. With my once lovely little chalkstream running at about fifteen knots, I sped downstream, crashing and lurching toward the Cottage Hole hatches.

Ahhh, bollocks! How could I have forgotten those?

There were three of them, all about five feet wide. Floating through them at normal flow would not have been too tricky, even on a twenty-six-foot bridge.

But not today.

My mind raced as I approached the Cottage Hole. I tried to

turn the bridge and point it downstream where it might actually pass straight through the hatches, but the current was too strong. It was going to be a broadside collision, and an ugly one at that.

I'm not sure if it was my life actually flashing before my eyes, but one indelible image remains in my mind: about twenty feet before impact, I caught a fleeting glimpse of those bastards from the Wildlife Trust. They were stood on the pathway with binoculars pressed hard to their faces and their mouths agape in alarmed wonderment. Whatever rare birds they had been watching were quickly forgotten as they trained their binoculars on the total prick of a riverkeeper barrelling downcurrent on a homemade bridge. Had they been surrounded by Dartford bloody Warblers, I doubt they would have missed this show.

Once again, caught in the act, I could think of nothing else to do other than give them my customary wave and grin. Unfortunately, my pathetic façade of sheepish confidence only lasted for another three seconds.

When the bridge slammed sideways into the structure, I was launched violently forward against the concrete barriers that straddled the river atop the hatches. I was lucky that the hatches held the bridge away from my body; otherwise I'd have been flattened like a fritter when the current welled up behind the bridge. Hanging on for dear life as the raging current battered my legs, I was finally able to slowly pull myself up onto the barriers and crawl across the hatches to the bank on the other side. The noise was deafening and the spray caused by the sudden blockage shot twenty feet into the air.

After lying there on the ground for a bit, wondering if in fact I was still alive, I slowly stood up and tried to wipe the mud and debris out of my eyes. It was raining, again, and I felt like a drowned rat that had just abandoned a sinking ship.

The binocular brigade was still standing, glasses affixed on my wretched image, and probably wondering what the hell I was doing in the first place. When they saw that I was indeed alive, they slowly wandered off to look for more very interesting birds. I could hear the laughter and they were shaking their heads with bewilderment as they walked around the corner and through the alders.

They'd got me again.

After a lot of heaving and tugging, I did eventually manage to pull the end of the bridge around, and once it was lined up properly with the hatch opening, it shot through as if fired from a cannon. For two pins I would have given it up, at that point, and let it wash out to sea, but then I decided that I had to get that bloody bridge to its intended spot. We'd been through a lot together and I wasn't going to give it up that easily.

Within seconds we were again doing about fifteen knots, and I winced with frustration as we sped past the little side stream where I'd planned to set up the bridge. Retrieving it to its intended position would now be an upstream pull, but first I had to stop its rapid downstream progress.

At the very bottom of my beat is a crossing called the Sea Pool Bridge. When the water is low, there's plenty of clearance between the bridge and the river's surface. On this day there was none, and that proved to be the only good luck that I'd found during this whole surreal experience.

Once again, my craft slammed sideways into the concrete bridge abutments and held fast in the current. After a bit of fishing, I was able to grab the rope that was tied to my bridge and slowly pull the end around. It took me nearly two hours of straining and pulling from the bank to walk it 100 yards back upstream to its intended spot. I was utterly exhausted by the time I finally got it lashed into place at the base of a big willow tree, and I collapsed onto its decking and lay in the pouring rain when the job was finally complete.

I fell asleep with the raindrops pattering on my face and when I woke up the rain had slowed to a drizzle. Dreading the long walk back to the house, I pulled myself up with an aching back and weary legs; I wasn't quite sure whether I'd actually make it or not, but the thought of a hot bath and a drink made me press on. I was convinced that I would bump into the binocular brigade again, but thankfully I was able to limp home unseen.

I was standing in the kitchen and stripping off my drenched clothes when my lovely Jo walked in and asked, "Darling, you haven't been out working in that rain have you?"

I tried to muster a suitable reply but nothing came. Not only had I been working in the rain, I'd done a bit of sailing, some basic gymnastics, a fair amount of load hauling, and a bit of comatose napping in a bloody downpour. All in all, I'd indulged in a public relations disaster and supplied the Wildlife Trust anoraks with an endless supply of joke material. Had I been out working in the rain? No, there was a bit more to it than that.

When Bama plodded into the kitchen and looked at his sodden master with obvious bewilderment, Jo nonchalantly asked, "Wouldn't just take him out for a quick walk would you, Love?"

Standing naked with steam rising from my knackered body, I looked down at Bama who had instantly recognized the "w" word and was now sitting attentively with that familiar *please, please, please* look on his face. It was getting dark and the rain was beating against the windows. Jo returned to her chair in front of the crackling fire, but she did make a half-hearted offer that I could see right through, "Of course, I'll take him if you're too tired."

I opened the door with a resigned feeling of inevitability and Bama charged out into the rain. Together we walked up to the top pool on the Little River. Neither of us had a stitch of clothing on.

Though not with the same feeling of freedom if attempted at your local park on a Saturday morning, I found that walking your dog in the rain while naked is fairly liberating.

After a few minutes of silent contemplation at the Lock Hatches Pool, Bama and I began to walk back toward the house. Though it was nearly dark and still raining, it was the only time I've ever been sorry that I *didn't* see those blokes from the Wildlife Trust staring at me through their binoculars.

The bridge is now secured in position alongside a breakwater called Lands End, and every time I cross it I remember its bizarre journey downstream and the suffering that I endured so that my fishermen don't get their feet wet. To date, though, what pains me the most about the whole sorry episode is the fact that nowhere on that bridge is there a shiny brass plaque to commemorate the event.

The Dead Cow Department

he banks of a Hampshire chalkstream are a great place to meet unusual and eccentric people from all walks of life. Over the past few years I've had opportunity to fish with all manner of humankind: the rich and the famous, captains of industry, sportsmen, politicians, and plenty of so-called celebrities. The great majority of them were very nice; even some of the politicians.

The one thing that they usually have in common, aside from the politicians bumming change for a fiver, is their parting comment regarding their perception of my work:

I would love to do your job; you're very lucky.

That may be true, but I wonder how many of them really appreciate or indeed understand exactly what my job is? For example, I am quite sure that most of my rods think that come the end of the fishing in September that I pack my bags and head off to the Seychelles, remembering to return just in time for the start of next season.

If only.

The most important part of any riverkeeper's duties, without question, is the task of keeping the river within its banks. On my beats at Nursling I am constantly adjusting, opening, closing, and clearing the hatches and the water mill. The gin-clear gently flowing river that most fishermen see during the season can in the winter months become a muddy raging torrent, and being held responsible for damage downstream can be a heavy burden to bear.

Opening a main hatch six inches drops the level of the river by an inch and a half, but if that same hatch is blocked, the water will rise at an alarming rate. Maintaining a constant level is a continuous game of open this one, close that one, with the river levels changing all the while. It's no so bad in fishing season, but during winter floods the hatches have to be monitored twenty-four hours a day. One pint of Guinness too many, forget to open a hatch and, *oh bollocks, I've just flooded Romsey.*

All sorts of rubbish and debris come down the river during flood and the hatches can block very quickly, and frequently do. I've had some strange things caught in the hatches and in the pools behind them. Telegraph poles are a favourite, as are life buoys, and the ever-present traffic cones. We get a seemingly endless supply of balls: footballs, tennis balls, beach balls, rugby balls and hockey balls—loads of balls. Lots of fly boxes come downstream along with hundreds of floatant bottles.

Occasionally, we get other less pleasant things—usually dead. I've fished cats, dogs, and sheep from the river, but they typically get through the hatches without problem. To date, the one farm animal that wasn't so cooperative was a dead and bloated cow that was stuck fast like a thousand-pound drain plug in one of my hatches. To drown in the River Test was bad enough, but this cow was also going to cop the blame for flooding upstream of my beat.

I decided to phone the Environmental Agency and asked for their flood defence department. Flood risk, or not, they didn't seem too interested in the removal of a dead cow and they passed me off with the usual, "Sorry, mate, not our department."

When I pressed a bit further they finally gave me a number for the Ministry of Agriculture, saying that cows were more their line of work. I agreed, although I did point out that the majority of their cows probably spent their time stood upright in fields and other cow-like places, and not tits-up in a river.

Eventually a man from the Ministry of Agriculture did arrive at Nursling Mill to inspect the offending blockage. After agreeing that it was indeed a dead cow blocking the hatches (and that it was really an EA flood response job), he begrudgingly agreed to remove it. He was a very nice man, but quite small, and I was intrigued by his yet unseen plan for removing the massive beast. He didn't have a big Land Rover with a winch; in fact he didn't seem to have any pulling equipment at all.

I followed him back to his car where he opened the boot. He then very carefully tucked his trousers into his socks, slipped his tie into his shirt, and pulled on a pair of brilliant white overalls. After pulling on some big green boots, he unfolded another pair of large overalls that he stepped into and zipped up. From there he added a pair of thick rubber gloves and taped them around his wrists for an airtight seal. His final line of defence was a large white helmet with a sealed visor that he placed atop his noggin.

After about fifteen minutes of methodical preparation, the spaceman appeared ready for the job, but I still couldn't work out how this little fellow was possibly going to remove half a ton of hideously bloated beef from one of my hatches.

Then he pulled out his chainsaw.

I don't want to go in to too many details, but he did remove the cow, albeit in several pieces. As you can imagine, his methodical preparation had not been in vain, and had obviously been learnt from many years of experience. I couldn't help thinking about that first unknowing apprentice from his department that was sent to do this same task.

Hey Joe, we need ya to pop down to the river and chainsaw a cow. Shouldn't take more than five minutes—here's a pair of gloves, you'll be fine.

After he'd left, I washed down the hatches and tried to clear off the footbridge as best I could. The smell was unimaginable and there were bits and pieces of cow all over the place. As I walked off the bridge back towards our exclusive rental apartments in the Nursling Mill, I noticed a new shade of pinkish, rather unusual looking pebbledash covering the entire apartment facade, windows and all.

Well, honey, you wanted to live in the country...

A Peaceful Summer's Day

rofessional fish poachers are a problem. They're good at their game and driven by the possible reward of cash in their pockets if they can sell their illegal catch. Fortunately, there aren't as many of them around as there were back in Vic's time, so nowadays I spend much of my time brawling with a different breed of nuisance.

Today, if I find someone fishing illegally on my beats, he's not likely doing it for financial gain; he's poaching because he's bored out of his dimly-lit skull. In general terms, today's trespasser comes in one of two flavours: the Irish gypsy or the local hoodlum.

Now, before I completely slag off those Irish vacationers that feel they have a right to fish my river without permission, it should be duly noted that I *am* of their descent. Apparently the Donovans come from Cork and people that come from Cork are more commonly known as "Bottle Stoppers," which is about as much knowledge of the Emerald Isle as I have so far mustered.

In fairness, however, I've also got some Hampshire blood, so they should get their critical due as well:

Hampshire born Hampshire bred, strong in the arm but thick in the head.

Unfortunately, that probably sums up the majority of local troublemakers who cause me much hassle in my daily work—at least the Irish go home now and again.

I would be pretty naïve not to expect kids on a river, especially during the summer months, but the majority of problems that we have are far more serious than people just messing about in the water. Times have changed since we were crafty kids trying to sneak a swim or catch the occasional fish using bread paste. Instead of old school poaching, their interests seem more inclined toward mindless vandalism and the seemingly endless pursuit of trying to make other people's lives as miserable as their own.

I've told the story of getting caught poaching on the Nursling beat as a youngster and having to walk a couple of miles to admit our guilt to the keeper. We were scared of getting caught doing anything wrong, and most of that fear came from the thought of having to go home and tell our dads. Actually being caught by a policeman was too worrying to even contemplate, and so the utmost respect was shown to everyone we met, let alone figures of authority. To be taken home nowadays by a policeman is something for a kid to be proud of.

I'm getting a bloody free lift from the cops; wait until I tell my mates about this!

I once caught a 12-year-old boy and several of his ilk attempting to break into my house using a screwdriver to lever open the door. I could quite easily have beaten this little villain but thought better of it and called the police to take him away. He was apparently a habitual thief who was well known to the police, although too young to charge. Because he was so young, his parents had to go to the police station to pick him up and I asked the officer if the boy would be worried about embarrassing his family. The policeman thought I was joking and explained that the boy's father, who was also well known to the local police, would probably come into the station and attempt to attack the boy—not for the attempted burglary, but for being stupid enough to get caught.

It was then that I began to understand that this lad was probably not such a little bastard after all, and the blame quite obviously lies with his upbringing and the attitude of his parents. What possible chance has any youngster got of growing into a decent law-abiding person under the influence of such parental behaviour? Absolutely none, and that total lack of respect for people and property from today's youngsters (and a few Irish) is the main difference between my time and Vic's.

What follows is a detailed account of a somewhat typical day's work during the peak season of fishing and hoodlum-ism. I now give you the events of August 8th, 2003:

9:00 am: I walk down to the bottom of the main river to confront six blokes about 25-years-old, all steaming drunk and fishing the river. I asked them to leave and they come back with the usual threats of retaliation, but they do leave.

1:30 pm: Trout fishermen complain of people in the river. I find two lads, about 20-years-old, walking up the river on the Trout Beat. I ask them to get out and leave, and they threaten to get out and break my legs. I call the police while the two twats walk downstream and join about twelve of their mates. I hide and wait for the police. Twenty minutes later and I'm still waiting, and hiding. All fourteen of the twats leave en masse. The police never show so I emerge from hiding and go home.

3:30 pm: A dog walker says there are about ten people fishing on my bottom bridge. I walk down and go through the usual routine of gentle persuasion and pointing out that the big "NO FISHING" sign did actually mean that you weren't supposed to fish.

4:10 pm: I get a phone call from my father-in-law who had just driven across the motorway at the top of the Trout Beat and seen two people fishing. Because they were spinning and had football shirts on he thought that perhaps they weren't supposed to be there. I walk up towards the Trout Beat —pissed off—and find two hoodlums in their twenties. One is drinking beer and the other is casting a spinning rod. He quickly puts his rod down when he sees me approach.

My action towards poachers has always been completely

determined by their attitude toward me, and as I walked opposite them on the other bank one of them said, between gulps of his lager, "Alright mate, can we help you?"

If they had just apologised I probably would have told them to clear off and not come back, but the wrong attitude was already present, and I felt something of a scuffle coming on. I strode toward them, weighing up which one was the fighter and which the talker. It's nearly always best to have some kind of plan in mind, either a plan of attack or discreet retreat. I must say, however, that some of my retreats from confrontations with the Irish have been anything but discreet. Legging it full pelt like a scolded greyhound may be the best option, but it probably doesn't look professional and it's certainly not discreet.

While they stood in the river and stared blankly at me, I asked the two poachers what they thought they were doing, a fairly stupid question with was followed by the predictable and equally stupid reply,

"Nothing."

After asking how they got onto the river, and why they had two spinning rods and a bagful of tackle, and why they had been casting their spinner across the river and winding it back, which suggested that perhaps, just maybe, they were trying to catch my trout, I again asked them what they were doing.

"Nothing; We ain't doing nothing."

"You mean *anything*, you are not doing *anything*, and not doing *nothing* means you must be doing *something*."

Sarcasm was lost, or rather, nobody likes a smart arse, so they just stood there staring with smug grins across their faces. I might still have told them to just bugger off, but then I found the fish, four of my trout in a Tesco's bag hidden in the undergrowth. People often tell me not to be so concerned, as after all they are only trout. I wish I could pass it off without incident, but I take it personally when I catch someone nicking my trout. A bit later the police turned up with the EA bailiffs and carted them away.

5:00 pm: Go to Testwood and give a statement to the police.

5:45 pm: More kids throwing stones and swimming on the Trout Beat.

6:05 pm: I send them off and they throw a couple of beer bottles at me as a kind of a going away present.

6:30 pm: I'm talking with the fishermen on the Drawing Room Pool, thinking that at last we've a little peace and quiet, when six local skinheads come casually walking up the bank towards us. The leader, scratching his head says, "Alright mate, where the bloody hell does this river end up, then?"

There he stood, his scratching time now being equally divided between his head and his balls, stupid grin on his face, "Made in England" tattooed on his bloated stomach, trying to act the big man in front of his mates. I shook my head at this embarrassing, self-proclaimed pathetic excuse for an Englishman and said, "Most rivers end up in the sea, but you're walking upstream, you prick."

Fighting is of course a ridiculous thing to do at any time in your life, and it does become more of a chore the older you get. For me it's the last resort and only a rare occurrence, although at times inevitable. I think that my sarcasm probably gets me into more trouble than it is sometimes worth.

Appearances can be deceptive when fighting is concerned and size of stature and of mouth does not necessarily equate to power of punch. I've usually found that the weaker ones typically do the most posturing and threatening. All mouth and trousers, they are. In a group they're in your face and full of bravado, but get them on their own and it's a very different story.

A good rule of thumb as far as fighting goes is to remember that one will walk, two will talk, and three will fight. But don't take that as a hardfast rule; I've been punched in the ear moments after shaking hands with a newly-made friend.

After a little altercation with the skinheads, they finally left, this time going downstream. The paying fishermen, who had been watching the proceedings with mild alarm, began packing their things to leave so I followed them back to the lodge.

If you don't drink whisky but have always fancied the idea,

become a riverkeeper over the summer months on the Lower Test and believe me, you'll get a liking for it. After the skinhead confrontation, I took a couple of slurps of the hard stuff and paused to watch the lovely summer evening draw in. Most people find joy in these placid and balmy moments, but not me. Nighttime is when the silly people come out.

Today, as with most summer evenings, I'm getting that nervous feeling in my stomach about the probable evening's entertainment with the local hoodlums.

Searching for Dutch courage at the bottom of a bottle, I turn into a fairly unsociable character at these times and tend to alienate myself from both friends and family. My wife calls me miserable during the summer because I pray for rain during the daytime and bad weather at the weekends—not for the garden or the river, but to keep the trouble at bay.

9:00 pm: After a few whiskies I'm ready for a trip down to the bottom of my beat to chuck off three nippers fishing on the Sea Pool Bridge.

10:30 pm: I take Bama for a walk up to the Trout Beat. Pretty sure I see a couple of people scurrying away.

11:30 pm: Go back on the Trout Beat and sit quietly in the dark and wait for the silly people to arrive. Although it's fairly pleasant sat on a riverbank in the middle of the night, it's not exactly relaxing, and although I'd rather be here than watching television, I must admit that this is usually the time that I often question the point of my existence. Luckily the silly people fail to show.

1:30 am: Fall into bed after another hot summer's day on the River Test at Nursling. Wonder if it will rain tomorrow?

I Can See You

he professional poachers who come out during the middle of the
night have one great advantage over us keepers: they haven't got
a life. Why is any forty-year-old man poaching for trout in the middle of
the night? Why isn't he in a pub drinking with his mates? Why isn't he
chasing women, or why isn't he making love to his wife—or somebody
else's wife for that matter? There must be something better for him
to do than poach my bloody trout. But, of course that's the whole
problem, he hasn't got anything better to do. He's got no mates, he
can't afford to go drinking, and his wife probably left him years ago.

Even though we keepers prefer to spend our darkened hours
doing more productive things, like sleeping, in recent years we
have taken advantage of available technology to help us catch the
sneaky bastards that steal our fish under the cover of darkness.

Night vision glasses.

These modern marvels have lately become the downfall of
many an old poacher who regards this technology as being almost
unsporting, and just not cricket. I'm afraid that in years to come
some poacher caught with night-sights will take his case to the
European Court of Human Rights. With the way that the law in this

country is going, we'll probably be banned from using them and have to pay *him* compensation for invasion of privacy.

In total darkness, armed with my night-sights, is probably when I feel the most at ease during my late-night poaching vigils. To be able to get within a few feet of someone fishing on your beat without them knowing is very exciting, and at times hilarious.

Looking through the night-sights is rather like switching the lights on, and at first I found them a little un-nerving to use as it seemed so bizarre to walk towards somebody who may be looking straight at me, but can't see me. I've seen the biggest, hardest poachers in Hampshire jump five feet in the air, scream like stuck pigs, summersault into the river, and do powerboat impersonations, all because I slipped up and tapped them on the shoulder in the pitch black darkness.

Another of my favourite tricks is to watch their reaction after I sneak within a few yards and make quiet little noises. Whispering, in particular, seems to put the fear of God into them and they'll typically make a hasty retreat, looking anxiously behind them. Some will stand their ground but will very often arm themselves with a stick or large stone and prepare for an attack by the unseen riparian boogieman.

The ones that do stand their ground are very often so relieved that it's only a keeper that they almost greet you with a welcoming hug before claiming that they had seen me all the while and were only having a laugh and playing along with my game. Others aren't so welcoming and are usually the ones who'll try to fight to regain a little pride.

Worse yet are the ones that run, but only after launching whatever they can pick up to defend themselves from the invisible monster. I can promise you, dodging airborne debris while looking through a night-sight is a dangerous game. Beer bottles seem a favourite means of ammunition, along with bricks, sticks, and rocks of all shapes and sizes. I've also dodged (or caught) clothing, tackle bags, footwear, a live hedgehog, and even the occasional trout, which makes me glad that we don't stock ten-pounders.

Most memorable was the local poaching bonehead that actually threw his fishing rod at me, which I caught in mid-flight and still have to this day. He obviously realised his mistake while the rod was arcing across the river. The final nail in his humiliation coffin was a pathetic apology, followed by "Mister, can I have my rod back?"

Unfortunately, while having things thrown at you can be dangerous enough, the real worry are the hoodlums that arm themselves more sincerely. A keeper on the adjoining beat was shot by a poacher and was lucky to survive. It seems surreal to be one moment talking of the peace and tranquillity of the chalkstreams, and in the next talking of an attempted murder. In truth, the wonderful serenity of the Hampshire chalkstreams comes with a price, a price that the riverkeepers often have to pay, and a price that not many of the fishermen ever see or indeed understand. Looking back, some of my dealings with poachers and trespassers now seem quite amusing, but being confronted daily by people intent on causing you physical damage can be an unsettling experience.

Beyond the physical confrontations, one of the worst threats aimed at keepers is the chilling, "We know where you live." statement. To worry about your own well-being is one thing; having your family threatened is an altogether different proposition. It almost seems unfair, but I try to keep my family completely away from the river and my job. I don't want any of the hoodlums to know which kids are mine and I don't like to mix my family life with the day-to-day running of the river.

Sadly, this defensive attitude begins to smack in the face of why I wanted to be a riverkeeper in the first place. It's typically a wonderful way of living in a lovely house by a river, bringing up a family in beautiful surroundings, but being at Nursling has not quite turned out that way. Nursling, in my view, is the best beat on the Test, but being down near the bottom of the river system means we are closer to so-called civilisation and its inherent problems. The summer, especially a hot one, brings out hordes of delinquent teenagers and midnight forty-year-olds. Over the ten-week period I feel almost separated from my family, like a virtual prisoner on the river, not daring to leave it for fear of what might happen.

September usually brings cooler temperatures and a return to school for the kids, which means that the troubles rapidly diminish. I love September and the onset of autumn, as it usually signifies a return to some form of normalcy: no more trespassers, no police, and no fighting. Even though I truly cherish my time with the anglers that fish Nursling (with permission), September also brings me a needed break from them as well. It's a wonderful time to be on the river: just me, the bridges, the breakwaters, and the fish.

The Tackle Tart

f the many things that are deliberately over-complicated, over-manipulated or elaborated to the point of idiocy these days, the fly-fishing tackle industry has to be at top of the tree. Sadly, it has become the place where the art of salesmanship and gullibility meet with the opening of wallets and closing of minds.

In theory, trying to catch fish with a fly rod is the simplest of things, and while observation, imitation, and presentation may be a concise way of describing it, those basic tenets have been hijacked by companies selling "must-have" dangles, bangles, and accoutrements. You need very little to fly fish for trout: a rod, a fly, and two bits of line in the middle. That's about it, really. From there, it's a matter of learning to cast, reading the water, a bit of entomology, and a lot of common sense.

It's a sad fact, but some people will simply never become great fishermen, no matter how much they try. Even worse are those who somehow think that lack of angling skill can be disguised by quality or quantity of equipment.

Early on, I learned that the anglers who arrive looking like fly-fishing catalogue models are very seldom as experienced as they look. Many times I have watched impeccably turned-out fishermen thrash the water into a frenzied lather and not only scare most of the fish in the Test, but a good deal of them in the Itchen, as well. I'm always amazed by those that arrive here with a half-dozen fine rods and a meticulous fixation on selecting just the right one for prevailing wind, moon phase, barometric pressure, and God knows what else.

I am no great expert on fly rods, but I've studied a number of the classic craftsmen, and I've built a few rods, myself. It's all about the correct balance. A fine rod paired with the right weight line is a pleasure to cast. That same rod fished with a mismatched line is about as effective as a 90-year-old widower on Viagra. Having a bloody great hard-on is totally useless if you've nowhere to go with it. No disrespect to 90-year-olds that *are* enjoying sex, but I hope I've made my point.

In addition to their unerring attraction to pricey rods and reels, the Tackle Tarts also come with a persistent affection for stylish clothing. We all have different thoughts on fashion and the way we'd like to look, but fishing is a sport where it's surely more important to dress for comfort and function, rather than appearance. Quite honestly, I couldn't give a toss how one dresses when they come to fish my beats, as long as they've considered the weather and they're not dolled up like an Eton Schoolmaster on a Boxing Day fox hunt.

In many ways I feel fortunate that I learned to fly fish from a master angler that held true to the minimalist theory that clothing and tackle really have very little to do with how well one presents a fly to a creature with a brain the size of a pea.

After a couple of dozen informal casting lessons in my early days at Martyr Worthy, Ron Holloway suggested that it was time for me to own a rod. I had saved up exactly one hundred pounds, and had not a penny more. Ron took me into the Rod Box, a quite famous tackle shop on the outskirts of Winchester, and we tried out a few rods whilst he gave a running commentary on each one. After selecting a rod, we chose a line matched to the rod weight and a simple reel. "No need to spend all your money on the reel," Ron suggested, "it's really nothing more than a line carrier."

After picking out a few flies, a priest, and a couple of leaders, we piled our goods on the counter where the merchant totted up the bill. I was astonished when he tapped the till for the final time and our total purchase popped up on the display.

"That'll be one hundred pounds, even," he said with a broad grin.

When I handed him my money in a crumpled pile, he straightened out the notes as he counted and then handed back a ten-pound note off the top of the pile. "Thank you very much, sir, but if you're fishing with Mr. Holloway, then you'll need some extra cash for a visit to The Chestnut Horse."

I still have that first fly rod and reel, and I'm very proud of the fact that I purchased it, within my budget, for the princely sum of ninety quid, plus a half-dozen pints of Bass.

Thou Shall Not Pass

t seems inconceivable that not too many years ago the Atlantic
salmon was seen by many people on the chalkstreams to be a real
nuisance. Some keepers treated them as vermin and many fish were
literally blown out of the water by those vigilantes and their trusty
twelve bores. Salmon, it was said, did not belong on the middle or upper stretches of the chalkstreams. They claimed that salmon only spoilt
the trout fishing by interfering with the spawning, attacking redds, and
generally bullying the poor old brown trout. It's sad to note that some
of the monster trout stocked into the rivers nowadays would probably dwarf the salmon; but back then they were a migratory pest in the
trout beats, and a general boundary of where the salmon fishing ended and trout fishing started was widely accepted on the chalkstreams.

Despite their intention of controlling the salmon's habitat, it
was eventually noted that while the fishermen and riparian owners found little difficulty in concluding what was a salmon beat and
what was a trout beat, the salmon wasn't quite as accommodating, and rather unsporting in the way that it refused to accept this
gentleman's agreement. The salmon, as it turned out, was innately
programmed to travel as far upstream as conditions allowed to find

the best possible spawning grounds. It was impossible to stop a natural urge that had been cunningly perfected over many thousands of years.

Salmon migration upstream is mainly governed by the volume and temperature of water. Beats higher up on the river systems obviously need plenty of water to encourage the salmon to keep running, while low water conditions suit the lower beats because that's where the fish will stop. I think that premise, as a rule, is generally accepted by most people as a fair explanation of salmon movement within river systems throughout the world.

On the River Test, however, the salmon apparently act differently and are being magically controlled by brilliantly clever riverkeepers who have learnt how to beat Mother Nature and hold the salmon on their own beats, irrespective of river conditions. Then once the fishing season has finished, these legendary keepers have learnt how to release the salmon to proceed upstream to find their spawning grounds.

I've always said we're underpaid.

We have all seen those wonderful wildlife programmes of salmon leaping seemingly vertical waterfalls with a determination that defies belief. The only way to manually stop a salmon's progress would be the construction of a massive hydroelectric dam (see the Western US for example). The River Test is not known for its waterfalls or cliffs, and at only forty miles long hardly represents a long slog for a fish that has travelled perhaps three thousand miles. Yet, still, there are keepers at the lower end of the river (including me) that are accused of skulduggery and in somehow illicitly holding the salmon back.

It's very important to distinguish between a keeper illegally blocking passage, and one making his beat attractive to salmon and providing a good and safe environment to encourage them to stay for a while. We can cut weeds in some places and leave it for cover in others. We can also maintain our breakwaters to create good holding pools. What we cannot do is manually impede the salmon's progress.

I have heard all sorts of ridiculous accusations ranging from blocking passes with wire mesh to hanging shark fins at the top of a beat that apparently no self-respecting salmon will dare to pass. The favourite accusation is that we shut the hatches at night and open them in the morning, although how people think that running the river bone dry below the hatches and flooding everything upstream is conducive to good salmon fishing, I've yet to understand. Unfortunately the easiest way of explaining a fishless day is to accuse the downstream beats of illegal tactics and in turning what was once regarded as myth and legend into something a little more menacing.

I'm all for a bit of banter and leg pulling between different beats, although some of the nonsense does at times go against the grain of everything we try to do for the survival of the Atlantic salmon. All that I want is for the salmon to reach its spawning grounds via the easiest, quickest, and safest route. I also understand the necessity of paying anglers to fund the upkeep of the river and for the likes of me to encourage a greater return of adult salmon. The balancing act of looking after both salmon and the rods is a difficult one, although with a little more subtlety with regard to fishing methods and with a little more sympathy towards certain ways of river management, this is easily possible, and something that Testwood and Nursling have actively encouraged for many years.

We are here primarily to look after the river and to safeguard the well-being of all its inhabitants—especially the salmon, and we cannot help but take offence when people upstream continue to make accusations of foul play. Where were these same people when we were working almost twenty-four hours a day on the brood stock programmes running fish about at all hours of the night? We have spent a considerable amount of time fighting everything from poachers to pollution, all in the cause of the Test salmon, but where were those people then? Probably fishing in Norway.

I remember one particular day in the winter of 2004 when I was woken at about 5:00 am by someone reporting poachers at the bottom of my beat. I crawled out of bed, crept down the frosted riverbanks to investigate, and chased off the poachers, but it ended with me escaping through the reed beds and narrowly avoiding a good kicking. Later that morning along with some Environment Agency people, I stood knee-deep in freezing water clipping adipose fins off of salmon smolts that were being released as part of the brood stock programme. It is quite a difficult job and my hands ached through the cold as the sleet beat down on our faces. When I finally got home that day I felt completely shattered.

As I was about to sit down for my dinner the doorbell rang and one of my children shouted that it was somebody to see me. I slowly pulled myself up from the chair and trudged towards the door, glancing at my steaming dinner on the table and holding my aching back.

My God it had better not be a bloody salesman.

It wasn't. It was a pompous man who, rather than introduce himself, barked that he wished to inspect the hatches on the Little River and to see for himself how I was holding back the salmon and selfishly keeping them at Nursling.

I was tired, hungry, and ached from head to foot after yet another day devoted to protecting and encouraging the very thing that this arsehole was accusing me of somehow harming. I stood there staring at him and toying with the idea of letting go the right haymaker I could feel clenched at my side. I tried to think of a worthy reply, but there wasn't one, so I closed the door and returned to the table.

My family was unusually quiet when I sat down to eat my dinner. They knew that the pompous man had touched a nerve. And whilst they had never seen him before and had no idea who he was, they knew that he was from somewhere upstream.

Motorcycles and Fishing Rods

or the past thirty years or so, my primary method of transportation has been an old British motorcycle. Sometimes it gets me halfway to my destinations, other times not quite that far, but it's no doubt a great little motorbike.

I've chased poachers on it and I've escaped from poachers on it; and while I'll admit to a few close calls, the bastards have yet to catch me. The one near miss with a pissed, shovel-wielding Irish gypsy did, however, prompt me to enquire about the chances of fitting an electric start button onto it.

An unusual "company vehicle" it may be, but I love my British bike, and am sure that it is to me what a cane rod is to the wicker basket brigade. Its attractions and our relationships can be similarly explained.

One of my mates has just bought a brand new 2004 Yamaha R1 motorcycle, and according to his normally sound judgement it is, apparently, the "dog's bollocks." It does nought-to-sixty in a little under three seconds and has a top speed of very nearly 200 miles per hour. It has incredible handling and amazing suspension, sounds like a grand prix car and looks like a space vehicle.

When the Yamaha R1 needs service, it has to be done by a team of professionals who plug it into a computer and tweak where necessary. Unless you have a degree in computer science and a Ferrari mechanic's toolbox, it's best you don't touch the engine bit. The R1 will start at the press of a button and is widely regarded by modern day racing lunatics as the finest and most exhilarating motorcycle ever made.

In my opinion, the 2004 Yamaha R1 is so brilliant, it's crap.

I ride a 1956 G9 Matchless, which fifty years ago was deemed to be of that same cutting edge technology. British motorbikes were the best in the world during that era and the Matchless was as good as any. Top speed for the Matchless G9 is about half that of the Yamaha R1. Comfort and handling are somewhat agricultural and your average modern day plastic-fantastic rider would probably get bored of waiting for its nought-to-sixty interval.

Of the many classic quips that I've heard from Vic Foot over the years, two apply to my motorbike: "Dangerous at both ends and uncomfortable in the middle," and "If it's got wheels or tits, you're bound to have trouble."

Starting the Matchless takes the strength of a carthorse, the balance of a gymnast, and the daring of a stunt man. If you get the timing of your kick-start slightly wrong, you'll be launched over the handlebars like an amateur cowboy. The Matchless is smelly, smoky, sounds like a machine gun, and leaves great pools of oil wherever, whenever, and indeed *if* ever you can stop it. It can be taken apart and reassembled at the side of the road using nothing more than an adjustable spanner, a decent screwdriver, and plenty of rags. Nothing too technical can go wrong with this bike because there is nothing very technical about this bike.

The 1956 G9 Matchless is so crap, it's brilliant.

Admittedly, I used to ride the motorbikes usually referred to by my Dad as "Jap crap." Like most kids, I was impressed with speed, acceleration, styling and so on. The older I get, however, I find myself more irresistibly drawn to the simplistic delights of an earlier time.

After many years of motorbiking up and down the Test Valley, I have noticed a difference in reaction relative to the machine I was riding. When I used to ride the quiet, clean, eco-friendly modern bikes, I sometimes felt an alarming sense of intrusion as I meandered my way through the delightful little villages. People would stare and scowl, and some would turn away in disgust. While I was never actually spat on, a few of the villagers looked as if they were considering it.

Nowadays, when I putter through the villages on the Matchless, sounding like a Sherman tank, scaring the living daylights out people and animals, and leaving a good deal of smoke in the air and oil on the road, I am looked upon as some kind of returning hero. *Oh look dear, a real motorcycle like the one Grandad used to have. They don't make them like that anymore.*

It's all about character, a bit of individuality, of style, feeling, and soul. The Matchless most definitely has a soul, and is a living, breathing, loudly-talking creation that has become much more than just a method of transportation; it has become a good, trusted companion. I have lengthy discussions with it, divulging personal information that I wouldn't dare share with anybody else. I understand the Matchless and feel as if I should look after it as I would an elderly relative. At times it becomes a temperamental old bastard that I cuss at when it refuses to start or breaks down at the side of the road; but just like in marriage, the making up part makes the fighting worthwhile. What on earth is the point in owning a bike that's never going to break down? Where's the fun in that? Half the enjoyment of owning the Matchless is in the promise that once in a while you may actually complete your journey on time and without having to rebuild the bike on the way.

If I could associate my adoration for the Matchless to a piece of fishing gear, it would have to be my preference for a classic bamboo fly rod over the modern-era carbon rods.

Like the flawless, gleaming Japanese motorcycles coming off the production line, the carbon blanks are mass produced overseas by machines that neither understand nor particularly care about the reasons why we fish.

Again it comes down to personal choice, and is very dependant upon how you want to fish, or indeed how you want to ride a motorcycle. Do you want to wear a full, snug leather suit with lots of colourful writing on it and go ridiculously fast at the touch of a button, or do you want to potter about on a misfiring old fart box while wearing goggles to keep the engine oil out of your eyes? Do you want to effortlessly cast forty yards using a piece of ultralight soulless carbon, or would you prefer to have a toned and muscular casting arm because you've chosen to fish with something that at one time in its life had leaves on it?

It's a tough choice that needs careful consideration, and probably should be decided well away from any elderly relatives, especially trout fishing grandparents who may claim to have ridden "real motorbikes" in their younger days.

With the motorbikes it's about whether you ride for enjoyment or necessity, although with fishing the same argument can't be used. Efficiency can never be measured against tradition because the Yamaha R1 or the carbon rod would win almost every time.

If we get pleasure from fishing with cane, then fair play to us. There's no need to pretend it's better than carbon because we're not trying to compete against carbon. Likewise, when sat at traffic lights desperately trying to keep the British bike ticking over, we never make grotty hand gestures at the Japanese models because us older, wiser people have finally realised that we don't want to race anymore, we just want to enjoy the ride.

I guess you could say that I've started defending the past. Strange thing, sentiment.

A Clash of Cultures

djacent to my beat at Nursling is a big lake that is chock
full with all manner of coarse fish. It's a public access that
typically attracts throngs of local sports, especially on the weekends.
Between the Test and that massive hole in the ground is a fence that
divides public property from private. It is indeed a dividing line for
access, but in many ways it is also a border between two societies.

The coarse fishermen refer to those that fish across the fence
as "Fluff Chuckers." From our perspective, they are the lowly "Maggot Danglers."

Of course, these nicknames were in place long before I arrived at Nursling, but I've often thought of them as generalised,
and even a bit misleading. Granted, us fly fishermen do at times
fish with fluff, but only on days when the insects are hatching and
the trout are rising. Beyond that, we're typically casting nymphs or
streamer patterns.

And, across the fence? Well, they do indeed fish with maggots,
but I can tell you straight up that on warm summer days I've caught
whiffs on the breeze from their bait buckets that were decidedly
not maggot.

So, while we've established that the "fluff" and the "maggot" bits are perhaps too narrow in their depiction of the actual offering that both groups present to their respective fish, there is yet another portion of these monikers that we must also address.

While we'd like to pretend that every fly cast we make is dead-on perfect, we do not always caress the line to the other side of the pool with an effortless flick of the wrist. Nor do we always engage that poetry-in-motion style of casting which becomes an art form to watch and a pleasure to perform. No, there is no doubting that a "chuck" slips in now and again, along with the obligatory "throw," the errant "launch" and the embarrassing "hurl." Fly fishing is not always as graceful a pastime as we'd like to imagine, and the effort that some require to get that stupid little bastard of a nymph or fly to the other side of the bloody river belies its gentle traditions.

Being called a Fluff Chucker by our coarse fishing brother anglers doesn't bother me one little bit. In fact, I consider it nothing more than a gentle tease from our maggot-dangling, worm-drowning, sardine-flavoured-boilie-bobbling, doze-under-a-bloody-bivvie-all-day *brother* anglers.

Many Fluff Chuckers are accused of snobbery and people always ask me if fly fishermen are as stuck up as they sometimes appear. Absolutely, of course they are—but it's not only coarse fishermen that they look down on. Snobbery is rife amongst fly fishermen and it depends on such utterly trivial things as price of rod, colour of waistcoat, and on which direction you prefer to cast your fly. Many fly fishermen are well and truly up themselves and wouldn't dream of using bread, unless of course it was wrapped around the appropriately sized Up-Winged Olive.

Thankfully the days of the chalkstreams being the exclusive playthings of Lords and Ladies have ended, and while it is still relatively expensive to fish for gamefish—and unfortunately out of reach for many younger people—the occasional passionate, working-class angler or coarse fisherman slips in and quite often turns out to be a fine fly caster.

To catch a certain species of fish you have to be able to think like that particular fish and a good coarse angler is much better equipped and prepared to do so. A coarse fisherman is far less likely to blindly fish through a pool hoping that something might just jump on the end without first giving thought to water conditions and where the fish are more likely to be.

I also think that some of the accomplished coarse fishermen eventually succumb to the temptation of a new challenge and progress from lakes through to rivers and then on to gamefish. They will quite possibly start their fly-fishing career on a hole in the ground filled with suicidal lumps of rainbow before progressing onto a river filled with slightly smaller and more athletic lumps of rainbow.

They will eventually work out that fishing for stocked trout in a pond is not quite as difficult as they had first imagined and then they'll go in search of wild fish in the streams. Some will return to the lakes, some will stick to the rivers, and others will eventually master both fly rod and conventional fishing.

The important thing, in my opinion, is that we are all brothers of the angle and must stick together and not create divisions between the various schools of fishing. That said, there is nothing wrong with a little banter between codes and leg pulling when appropriate.

On a recent Saturday morning, I was wandering the riverbanks and came to the fence separating the Test from the aforementioned hole. It was surrounded by Maggot Danglers trying to win twenty-five quid by catching Queenie, the resident behemoth carp that, on average, eats a dangled bit of smelly something about seven times each fortnight. I've never really understood the attraction of match fishing. To me, the whole point of fishing is to avoid the problems that competition inevitably brings, especially when money is involved.

On this particular morning the lake looked like an unruly Boy Scout camp, or perhaps a staging area for a team of climbers making a summit push on Everest. As I stood marvelling all of the tents, sleeping bags, camp stoves, rods, and bait buckets, a voice called out to me from the horde, "How you getting on my old Fluff Chucker—caught many spotties have we?"

I stood and watched him add another knackered dace to his bulging keepnet before I answered, "No mate I haven't caught any spotties—in fact I haven't had a cast, nothing rising yet, but I hope it will be good this evening."

"So you just wander up the riverbank and you haven't even fished yet, where's the fun in that? Bloody Fluff Chuckers, why don't you just give in and use bait—dog food would be great for trout."

I had about one and a half miles of glorious riverbank all to myself, and this fellow was sat around a hole with twenty others, and he couldn't understand how I could possibly get pleasure from just wandering. It had nothing to do with money or a them-and-us feeling, we were just two blokes fishing our respective ways. He and his mates were quite obviously very happy—and fair play to them. But each to their own, because while we may indeed be brother anglers, there are often insurmountable barriers between us and a bemused stalemate of misunderstanding.

So there at the convergence of two societies, with the fence firmly stood between his fishing world and mine, I shrugged my shoulders and replied, "I've tried dog food, mate, but I can never get the hook to stay in the bloody can."

A Fisherman's Seat

y wife, Jo, has a fancy for incessantly rearranging the furniture in our front room. I suppose it's a congenital thing among women because I've compared notes with a lot of other men and their wives were all born with the same dragging and scooting inclination.

On a whim she'll move the armchair to the other side of the room and the television over next to the lamp. When I say *she* will move it, I obviously mean that she will ask *me* to move it, or rather *tell* me to move it. Then the sofa has to be dragged over to the wall opposite the fireplace with the bookshelf facing the other direction, and so on. Then it will all be moved back again the following month and repeated on an almost non-stop basis.

This annoyed me greatly when we first married, yet I've become much more tolerant of Jo's affinity for furniture moving since I began building seats on the riverbank at Nursling. I now understand exactly where she is coming from and our marriage and love for each other have become much stronger. Just her nod in the general direction of the sofa will now have me pushing it around the front room with the kids still sat on it; as long as the television moves in unison they never even notice that they're underway.

My newfound conclusion is that the positioning of the sit-on furniture, whether a chair in the front room or a seat on the riverbank, is absolutely fundamental to enjoying a nice sit-down.

Building a seat next to the river is not quite as simple as you might at first imagine. The construction of the seat is easy enough, especially with my mastery of intricate chainsaw joinery. Unlike bridge building, a typical Nursling bank-side seat consists of very little wood so the logistics involved in getting material onsite are easily overcome; no river rafting required.

The real essence of a good seat is in the positioning. It might only take me half an hour to build a seat from start to finish, but before the first nail has been driven, I will have studied the proposed area of construction from every conceivable angle. I will have viewed the jobsite from across the river, from upstream, from downstream, and occasionally from a tree limb to gain the aerial perspective. Too close to the water, not enough room to get the mower past, directly opposite a good salmon lay, wrong backdrop, sun in the eyes—there are many things to consider, any of which if wrongly chosen will render the seat useless.

Once I've decided on the position of the seat, the actual construction requires a fourteen-pound sledgehammer, a chainsaw, four six-inch nails, and a hammer. A spirit level seems like an elaborate addition to my rather sparse tool kit, but getting the top of the seat level is imperative. The height of the seat is also important and I've learned over time that nineteen inches from the ground to the top of the seat is the magic number. It doesn't matter how tall or how short you are, eighteen inches is too low to the ground and twenty inches is too high.

Once the measuring and cutting are done, the process is quite simple. Using the big sledge, I'll first pound the two uprights into the ground to a depth of at least two feet. That depth is important, not only for stability, but to deter the local hoodlums from pulling them up and tossing them in the river. No, they haven't got anything better to do.

Since I use 2x8 boards for the actual seat plank, I'll then use the chainsaw to cut off the uprights to exactly seventeen inches. With four six-inch nails I'll then hammer the 2x8 plank into place atop the uprights, and it's done!

If feeling especially charitable, I'll sometimes use the chainsaw to shave off the sharp edges, but that's as far as I'll go. Sandpaper is out of the question as I'm far too busy to spend extra time pandering to the doughy white arses of the Nursling fishermen.

I love building seats.

Along the banks at Nursling there are probably a dozen such seats, and I spend many hours each year sitting on and testing each and every one of them just in case they've skewed slightly from their once-perfect angle. I know that might sound eccentric, yet I assure you it's an important part of my job.

There are one or two slightly more substantially built seats at Nursling, including my favourite, which I've modestly named "The Best Seat in the World." This marvel of modern engineering is situated at the head of the Drawing Room Pool and looks downstream following the Little River on its meandering journey through the water meadows. Construction of this seat is a little more detailed than your average bankside model and the sculptured privet hedge that surrounds it gives it an air of the Kew Gardens.

Over the years, The Best Seat in the World has become a great time waster with the Nursling anglers. Instead of fishing they'll spend great amounts of time sitting, eating, smoking, drinking, and at times sleeping on it. A few years ago a young couple also spent plenty of time there, although from the positions they seemed to get themselves into, I'm not sure they realised it was a seat at all.

My latest addition to the Nursling seat collection has only just been unveiled (patent pending) and if I say so myself it has become something of an instant classic. It stands alongside the fishing lodge and I'm sure will in time become a famous Nursling landmark. The only downside is in its weight, which I'd estimate at about half a ton, perhaps slightly more. I have attempted to justify both its weight and size as part of the security plan, and if any hoodlum is strong enough to actually carry it away, then they're probably too strong for me to stop them from stealing it. The real reason for its excessive bulk is that I got too excited during construction and kept adding unnecessary bits, such as the magnificent rod holder on the back (up to eight rods) and a pair of elegant, if perhaps extravagant armrests.

Not being particularly experienced at the intricacies of waterproofing, I now know that slathering it with creosote was a mistake, and would like to apologise to the large gentleman who fished at Nursling this year and became the first to christen the new seat. When he got home, he must have wondered where all the extra black stripes on the back of his new tweed jacket had come from. Next time I'll just stick to the positioning and construction details and avoid painting and decorating.

Incidentally, I've since sold one of these seats for two hundred quid and word of its marvellous and innovative design has travelled rapidly throughout the Test valley.

Only five thousand more and I'm a millionaire!

The Angling Celebrity

've never been impressed with the word "celebrity" and even less so with people who think of themselves as such. Now, granted, some have rightfully earned that title after long and prosperous careers in acting, writing, hitting a ball, singing, etc. Yet there are others within those same fields who are really only famous for being complete arseholes. Indeed, I think that the number of times the words "celebrity" and "arsehole" are used in the same sentence is probably more than just coincidence.

It has become quite the fashionable thing among the celebrity set to fly fish on the Hampshire chalkstreams, yet many of them are there more for the photo-ops than the fishing. In their view, fly fishing is a cool thing that makes for great party talk and a trendy addition to their curriculum vitae. If only those slimy fish weren't involved.

Instead of lumping all famous people who fish into a single category, we should probably look more closely at the subtleties and genres. First we have the angling celebrity as described above; the renowned actor, author, or athlete who also fly fishes (and typically not very well). Opposite that group are the celebrity anglers;

the so-called professional fishermen who are on television, video, magazine covers, etc. I have witnessed the making of many fishing programmes and have seen plenty of these angling gurus in action. A common thread among them is not so much their angling prowess, but an innate love of hearing their own voices.

As you might guess, through the use of staging, editing, duplicating, and other smoke and mirror tricks, what we see on television as the final production is typically nothing like the actual events that transpired on the river. With the current popularity of reality television, I wish we could have a weekly fishing programme where the celebrity angler fishes the best waters around the world and catches bugger all. The final scene should have him walking dejectedly away from the water trying to convince himself that catching fish doesn't really matter and there's no such thing as a bad day out of doors.

Now, that'd be a real ratings smash, wouldn't it?

The angling celebrity, on the other hand, is usually not particularly bothered by a fishless day. For them it's more about the Range Rover and the pricey accoutrements that being a fly fisherman allows them to own. It's being able to tell the magazines that they can be found fly fishing while relaxing between projects.

Interestingly, however, some within this set will really take to fly fishing, and over time they'll invest in the practice, details, and techniques required to master the sport.

Even though I'm always leery of them up front, angling celebrities that have transformed into accomplished rods have become some of my favourite to fish with.

In May of 2005, one of my season rods phoned me to explain that he couldn't make it on a certain scheduled day and that he was sending a guest, instead. He added that I would instantly recognise him as he was a famous actor. Of course, without even hearing the name I had already made up my mind that I wouldn't like him, but my job required me to feign the necessary interest.

"Geoffrey Palmer," he said, as I remained silent. "You know, Geoffrey Palmer? He was in *Butterflies* with Wendy Craig."

After another ten seconds of silence which undoubtedly broke his spirit, I replied, "Ahh yes, the bloke who's in *Only Fools and Horses.* I know who you mean."

"No, no, that's David Jason, you'll know this man when you see him, he's really famous. He's coming next Tuesday, I've given him your mobile number."

I felt confident that I had burst his bubble and I didn't give it another thought until Tuesday arrived and my mobile phone rang from its safe place down the front of my trousers. I keep it on silent mode while fishing and the vibration down front is the only pleasure I get from the bloody annoying apparatus.

"Hello, this is Geoffrey Palmer. Are you Donovan?"

I thought for a second of telling him that he had just made my bollocks tingle, but decided instead to play it cool. "You must be Palmer, I've been expecting you and, *no*, this is not *Donovan*. It's *Martin* Donovan or *Donny* to most people."

"Oh I'm sorry, Donny, how very rude of me. I was told that your name was Donovan. I'm outside your house and just wondered where I should park."

At that point I felt like an offensive and arrogant git for snapping at him when it was obviously a simple miscommunication. He was smiling with his hand outstretched when I found him standing next to his car. He apologised again, as did I, profusely.

From that moment on, celebrity or not, Geoffrey Palmer and I got on like a house on fire. He has that same fascination for the rivers as I do, and he told me that one of his biggest regrets was that he started fishing relatively late in life. We wandered down the Little River and the barrage of questions made me feel like a schoolteacher with a new and enthusiastic young pupil. He was very keen to learn about our nymph fishing techniques for salmon and seatrout, so we set his rod up with a weighted nymph and took along plenty of dry flies in case there was anything rising.

After one or two lessons with the weighted nymph, he took the rod and fished a few of the breakwaters as we walked downstream. When we got to the Navvies Shovel, a beautiful breakwater about two-thirds down the Little River, he hooked a magnificent seatrout of about five pounds and was absolutely giddy of his accomplishment.

After releasing the seatrout, we went a little further down and sat on the old hatches of the Cottage Hole Pool and watched the mayflies begin to break out on the surface. The weighted nymph was taken off, leader changed, and a Grey Wulff tied on. Fishing our way back upstream, we caught some chub, a few beautiful wild brownies, one or two dace, and another spectacular bright seatrout on the dry fly. It was a day that a ghillie dreams about where an enthusiastic angler is afforded an opportunity to fish a great stream full of cooperative fish.

When we got back to the fishing hut we had a cup of tea and a sandwich and sat talking about the Nursling beat, salmon fishing in Scotland, and the problems facing the salmon at sea. Not once did he talk of television or stardom, nor did he drop names or brag of his fame. He was quite content sat in a fishing hut eating a cheese sandwich and talking to the keeper about fishing things.

Geoffrey is an excellent fly fisherman and has renewed my limited faith in angling celebrities. He has made me think twice before prematurely marking somebody down as a probable arsehole just because they have a recognisable face.

The Demonstration

t is, of course, a well-known fact that most of us who live and
work on the rivers are excellent fishermen and not averse
to a little showing off now and again. Not only should the ghillie
or riverkeeper know the water better than his client, but the job
description also requires that he should out-fish and out-drink his
sports, as well. If you ever pass your rod to a Scottish ghillie after
completing the longest cast of your life, he will without fail pull off
a few extra handfuls of line before casting ten yards past your best
mark. It's also best not to get too involved in selecting a proper fly,
as we will inevitably reject your offering, even if we know it'll work.

I am of course exaggerating, and you will very rarely find
anybody who works on the river with such a high opinion of
themselves, though there are a few. More prevalent, however, are
the fishermen who take great delight in trying to catch the keeper
out by asking particularly daft and obscure questions in the hope
that just maybe he won't know the answer. That may be a question
about an unusual fly or some ambiguous plant growing on the riverbank, but there is no doubting the smug look if you don't know
the answer.

If people ask me about a plant that I'm not familiar with, then I'll typically just make one up. Using a Latin name seems to work particularly well. *Conium Maculatum* (Hemlock) is the one I normally use, and thus far no one has questioned it. Incidentally, that particular name also works well for identifying unknown birds, reptiles, insects and trees.

One of the great difficulties that keepers and ghillies have is getting their clients to actually see the fish before they cast to it. It's not too difficult on bright sunny days when the fish casts a shadow on the bottom, but it can be quite tricky when there's no sun and the client doesn't understand the concept of looking through the water, rather than looking at it. Many times I have been pointing out salmon to a fisherman who just cannot see it, and the only solution is to act as their eyes and guide them in. Here is an exchange with a first-timer that fished with me at Nursling this past summer:

"Cast towards that bush alongside the ranunculus, sir, and let it drift down. Throw a little bit of slack upstream to give the nymph a bit more time to sink. Try and get a bit closer to the bush, sir. Never mind, a bit too close perhaps, don't worry I've got another one in my pocket. Try again, sir. Oops, still a bit close, yes they're two quid each, I've only got one left. Try her again…okay, then, that's better, let it drift…and…lift it….now."

When the salmon left his lie and moved toward the nymph, the angler leapt into the air and shouted, "My God Donny there's a bloody great salmon down there, did you see it?"

"Yes sir strangely enough I did see it, that'll probably be the same one that I've been pointing to for the past twenty minutes."

Suggesting flies, identifying flora and fauna, and pointing out fish are the easy bits for those of us who make their living guiding anglers. We do, however, walk a fine line between teaching and criticising, because there is one challenge from our sports that we fear more than any. It typically comes from the frustrated angler that just can't seem to make the connection between fish and fly.

Well come on then, Mr. Expert, you come and show me how to catch one.

Any keeper, by virtue of his time on the water, is bound to be relatively good at fly casting, but actually parlaying a good cast into a caught fish is more difficult because you are dependant on a third party; a fish that may not be in the mood to bite a dressed hook.

Catching a fish on cue from a stocked trout beat is usually not much of a problem. Salmon and seatrout, however, are a completely different game, especially when there aren't many in the river.

In the summer of 2005 I was presented that dreaded challenge by a group of six fishless rods on a particularly hot and still day. After a fruitless morning of whipping the river into froth, they practically begged me to show them how it is done and to reassure them that they were at least fishing correctly. Though not great fishermen, they were all very nice people, so I was more than happy to give the advice for which they asked.

I took my rod from the wall and we all wandered down to the river like a mother and her six little ducklings. Had I stopped quickly they all would have piled into the back of me, such was their keenness to keep up. We walked about a hundred yards downstream from the Drawing Room Pool to the second breakwater down, which is rather strangely called the First Breakwater. It's a small pool with excellent holding water for salmon, and the perfect place to demonstrate the weighted nymph technique. When we arrived, they all lined up in formation along the bank to watch the proceedings.

One of them, the self-appointed leader of the duckling troupe, had fished for trout on the Test for many years and was much more experienced than the others. They had all fished this same pool earlier in the day with no luck, and now felt that there was quite obviously nothing in it. The leader only added to the anticipation by slowly shaking his head, as if daring me to catch a fish in a place that he had fished methodically from top to bottom only an hour earlier.

Taking a couple of handfuls of line off my reel I turned to face my pupils, who were watching my every move. All of them, that is, except the leader, who was studying the orange balsam next to the river, making the point that he needn't listen to every bit of advice;

he was only there out of courtesy and would pick up a few bits and pieces, if needed.

I roll casted about twelve feet of line directly upstream of the breakwater and began a running commentary of what I was trying to do and why I was trying to do it.

"Let the nymph sink to the end of the leader so that the fly line is on top of the water and let it come down about a third of the pool before stopping the rod and so causing the nymph to slowly rise to the top."

As the nymph slowly came to the surface a beautiful grilse rose from the depths like a silver torpedo and nailed it about two feet from the top. My pupils were stunned. I carried on my commentary as if it was all part of the lesson and something that I had fully expected to happen.

"When the fish takes it like that it's very important to lift into him and really set the hook. It's also important to play them from the reel, keep downstream of them, and don't give them too much line. If they run then you must follow them; give them too much line and they'll be gone."

I tried to pass the rod to one of my startled pupils, but none of them wanted to take it. After a couple of minutes I asked somebody to net the fish for me and, of course, the leader wished to demonstrate his netting prowess. As I guided the fish towards the net, he made the mistake of reaching too far for it and stepped through the reeds straight into eight feet of water. He managed to scramble, gasping and sputtering, back onto the bank where he finally netted the grilse.

The fish was immediately unhooked and released to the river, and I finished my lesson with, "And that gentlemen is how we fish the weighted nymph at Nursling."

When they were finished staring, they all thanked me and carried on downstream to put their newfound knowledge to the test. I walked back to the fishing lodge with a confident swagger and a spring in my step that I was careful not to let them see, knowing that I would probably never be able to do that again.

After all, everybody admires expertise, but nobody likes a smart arse.

The Missing Pike Heads

y father was an annoyingly brilliant debater who could win any argument using nothing other than quietly-spoken common sense. It was not unusual for him to momentarily swap sides halfway through an argument, lend support to my point of view to even things up a little, and then revert to his original point of opposition and inflict another humiliating defeat. I never once got the better of him, but I look back on those discussions fondly, and I learned a lot from each trouncing.

I still love debate, and those maddening sessions with my father taught me that listening to the opinions of others is equally as important as voicing your own. He also taught me that I should always be open to changing my opinions and admitting defeat when necessary.

Fortunately, I've been able to apply those lessons during my career and they have influenced many of my thoughts on fishing and riverkeeping, in general. Being able to graciously accept a different, more valid point of view from somebody who I consider a complete bastard has helped me look after the river through the harsh realities of the twenty-first century without worrying over losing face.

Accepting change, these days, often means that I'm turning my back on age-old tradition and questioning the necessity of certain working practices which are done solely because "it's always been done like that."

Management of the river itself is not the only place where I've readily accepted changes in practice; my moral attitude toward such things as catch and release and the management of certain predators also differs from that of the older generations.

The keeper's cottage in which I now live at Nursling is famous for the pike heads nailed on the rod room door by those who lived and worked here before me. The pike heads were something of a local attraction when I was a boy, and on the day that I had to answer to Vic for poaching his trout, I can vividly remember studying the heads of those vicious monsters who'd have my leg off if I dared venture into the river.

Nowadays there are only two remaining heads on the door and those are in the last stages of their skeletal life. People often ask if there are no longer such monsters in the river, or perhaps if the current inhabitant of the fishing cottage is not such a master at snaring them? The answer probably includes a little of both, but the main reason for the lacklustre display of predators on the door is that I no longer kill the pike. We still catch plenty at Nursling, but nowadays they're transported live to more welcoming water, usually lakes near to the river, where they can thrive and also give sport to other fishermen.

I suppose, really, that I'm just a big softie who can see no point in killing such a beautiful fish for very little purpose other than proving that I'm doing my job. I can remember walking around some of the great shooting estates with my grandfather and being astonished at the numbers of "pests" strung up along the fences adjacent to the keeper's cottages. There were hundreds of dead moles, jays, crows, magpies, and squirrels lining the fences in immaculately straight rows like medals proudly displayed on a brave war veteran's chest.

I feel a little guilty interrupting such a long and treasured tradition as nailing pike heads to the fishing cottage door, and I can understand people thinking it's a shame that things are not as they once were. I do hope, however, that in the longer term perhaps people will understand that we must change with the times and, dare I say, adopt a more sensitive and understanding approach.

Compassion for the fish, however, is not the only reason that I no longer kill every pike I see. I have also noticed, over the years, that it makes very little difference how many pike are removed from the river because there's always another to take the place of the most recently dispatched. Kill a pike from a certain swim and the next day its identical twin will have taken up the same lay. I feel it's much wiser to leave the bigger ones in the river and let them run the neighbourhood clear of the jacks. They can control their own numbers much more efficiently than any keeper ever could, and once the bigger ones become too many, we transplant a few of them to more receptive water.

Other, less threatening coarse fish also inhabit my beat at Nursling, all of which are a pleasure to see in the river. Apart from a few of the older generation, most Nursling anglers like to see different species, whether carp, bream, chub, grey mullet or seabass. I'm hearing, now, that fly fishing blokes in the United States are going absolutely batty for carp. Perhaps there's another untapped cash flow (albeit an ugly one) lying amidst my prized trout and salmon?

Keepers today are also much more tolerant of avian predators than in past generations, and a kingfisher is now regarded as a special sight on the chalkstreams. Would I want a couple of hundred kingfishers at Nursling? No; but thankfully nature has a way of making sure that won't happen. Herons and (God forbid) cormorants are also a common sight on my beat but, again, those are predators that I prefer not seeing in too great a quantity.

Otters were at one time hunted to near extinction in the Test Valley, but now we're occasionally thrilled to see one at Nursling. I feel that we should accept that natural predators have much more right to inhabit the riverbanks than any fly fisherman. And, honestly, who can begrudge an otter taking the occasional trout?

The natural predators do have an effect on game fish numbers, but these days they have actually become the least troublesome to the chalkstreams. Abstraction and pollution are now greater threats, along with the water companies and their constant haggling for flow rights. If only there were a license that we keepers could purchase to cull a few of *them* from the river, each year.

I think it important to change with the times and accept that just because something has been done a certain way for the last hundred years does not necessarily mean that it's right. To be someone who attempts to change tradition means having a thick skin, because ridicule and derision from some quarters will undoubtedly follow.

Partly due to a general acceptance of more eco-friendly thinking, and partly because of the dramatic decrease in numbers of predator species, I have no problem in explaining to people, probably a dozen times every summer, why there are only two old pike heads left on the fishing cottage door.

Unfortunately, the missing pike heads do trouble me when I see the look of disappointment in the eyes of children that have been brought to see the monsters by dads who'd been brought by their fathers, before. Perhaps I should mould a few of them from papier-mâché.

Americans

O n one of my first days working at Nursling, I was walking
the riverbank with Vic Foot who was pointing out and nam-
ing plants as we passed them. Even though he knew much more of
the foliage than me, there was one particular plant name that I knew
to be wrong. Being so new on the job, it felt awkward to correct him,
so I decided to accept it for what he said. The plant in question was
Himalayan Balsam, which Vic referred to as "American Balsam."

Months later when I finally plucked up the courage to question his identification of that plant, he casually said that he knew
the correct name was Himalayan but had always called it "American" because of its certain characteristics. It was, he explained,
very invasive and stubborn, and once it gets a foothold it's almost
impossible to get rid of before it finally takes over the whole bloody
neighbourhood.

American Balsam it is, then.

From 1983 to 1988 I spent quite a lot of time living and
working in America and have travelled literally thousands of miles
passing through some forty-two different states. I love America and
a good deal of its inhabitants. It is strange, therefore, that I feel an

unfair sense of inevitability when I say that on average the best fly fishermen (and tackle) that I encounter are very often American.

A lot of Americans come to fish the Test and I have had the pleasure of guiding some of them on the Nursling beat. Their personalities do vary, but the one thing that is always immediately apparent is they can all fish well and are usually excellent casters. This of course helps while in the pursuit of fish, but what also differentiates them from other rods is their intensity and quest for knowledge. They literally batter you for information.

There are many other differences between the English fly fisher and the American, some subtle, some sledgehammer, but the most noticeable to me is that while the Englishman begrudgingly listens to my advice so that he can completely ignore it, the American comes here looking for fishing advice and will actually apply it. The American will tie on the suggested fly and trim their leader to whatever length I tell them. If after half an hour he hasn't caught, he'll often come back to find me and ask for other suggestions. The Englishman on the other hand, will politely ask my advice, do the complete opposite and casually wander off to catch nothing all by himself, having avoided the ignominy of having to be helped.

While we do see a lot of Americans on the chalkstreams, most of them seem inclined to visit only once. Perhaps, for them, it's more of a pilgrimage to the origin of fly fishing, rather than the quality of the actual fishery. I remember going to visit Stonehenge and feeling somewhat let down when I realised that it was indeed only a pile of bloody great rocks in the middle of a field. The roar of juggernauts blasting past on the A303 on the other side of the barbed wire fence didn't exactly help the mystique that I had so associated with Stonehenge. It was better in my mind than in reality and, with so many great trout rivers in their home states, I suspect that many Americans may feel the same when they come here to fish.

Another interesting trait of Americans is their brutal and upfront honesty. Whether it be fishing, politics, sports, religion, or culture: they simply tell it like it is. Cut and dried with no grey areas.

———

Of all the places I've visited in America, I've spent more time in Alabama than any other state. Alabama is roughly the same size as England, with the friendliest, most polite people that I have ever met.

There is a small piece of coastline in Alabama that fronts the Gulf of Mexico and the beaches are as nice there as they are in neighbouring Florida. Alabama, it seems, is thought of as a rather poor relation to the rest of America and people always look fairly startled when I tell them that it's my favourite state. Most Americans think of Alabama as being full of stoned rednecks, and while I agree that there are a lot of them, it's not only the rednecks that are stoned; most of the policemen are, as well.

My journey to Alabama began while hitchhiking on the outskirts of Chicago in 1984. I was picked up by a rather unusual looking vehicle painted an extraordinary shade of purple, and towing a large trailer. It was a Winnebago with Alabama license plates, and the driver gave me the thumbs-up as he pulled over to offer a lift. His name, he proudly announced, was Keys Mitchell and he produced a business card that he pushed into my hand.

He reminded me a little of the so-called doctors that travelled throughout the Wild West selling lotions and potions, pulling teeth, and cutting hair all at a reasonable rate. He was in fact a grandfather clock salesman travelling all over America doing shows in shopping malls and country fairs. After only a few minutes, I had been thoroughly apprised of the virtues of his wonderful clocks and the deals he could offer.

He worked for The King Arthur Grandfather Clock Company and was based in Fairhope, Alabama. Keys would travel from mall to mall and set up his sixteen clocks that he carried in the trailer. He lived in the Winnebago and explained that everything associated with the company, including his suit, was painted in this extraordinary shade of purple. We got on like long lost friends and, like a lot of Americans, he talked as if it were his last day on earth.

We travelled throughout the Southwest and I helped him do

shows in Phoenix and Flagstaff. We visited the Grand Canyon and it was strange to see Indians (as in cowboys and Indians) riding along just like in the olden days. I was surprised that Keys didn't attempt to trade guns and liquor with them, but apparently he was only into clocks.

I eventually ended up working with Keys and selling the clocks, and I found it one of the easiest jobs imaginable. Working as a team, we sold literally dozens of them.

After quite a time on the road, we worked our way back to Alabama to the clock company factory where we were summoned to meet the owner, George Fowler, to presumably explain the sudden upturn in sales.

After waiting in the sales office for a nervous half hour the door suddenly burst open and in rolled this enormously fat man in a wheel chair with a secretary hurrying behind him. I stretched my hand out toward him, but he just stared at it, so I awkwardly scratched my nose instead.

"You the Limey bastard who's been selling lots of my clocks?" He had a booming voice and a distinctive southern drawl. "Must be you, because I know it ain't Keys. He couldn't sell his ass in Alcatraz."

Before I had any chance to reply he shouted another question, "You know, Limey, what I miss most about being in this goddam chair?"

A thousand things flashed through my mind in a millisecond that this large and noisy man may have missed by being in a wheelchair, but I didn't have time to respond before he answered, "Having a good crap. That's what I miss more than anything, taking a damned good crap!"

I just didn't have an answer. I didn't know whether to agree with him, sympathise, or what. To be perfectly honest I'd never given the subject of not being able to go to the toilet much thought and I was, therefore, lost for conversation.

No such problem for Keys, though. This was his kind of subject. I waited with gritted teeth and closed eyes for his inevitable intrusion.

"What about masturbating, Mr. Fowler?" Keys asked, "I'm sure that I'd miss that more than crapping."

"Well you would, Keys, and you wanna know why? The Limey's got a word for you where they come from. A *wanker*. In England you're a *wanker*. Ain't that right Limey? In England, Keys is a wanker, ain't he?"

Keys was now in his element, so I wasn't the least surprised when he replied, "So let me get this right, George. I'm a wanker and you're full of crap because your asshole doesn't work?"

There was a long silence, and I couldn't quite tell if it was checkmate, stalemate, or what...but it was very quiet. Without a word, Mr. Fowler suddenly wheeled and turned to leave the room, nearly knocking his secretary over in the process. As he once again crashed through the doors he shouted back toward me, "Come see me tomorrow Limey, I got big plans for you!"

We picked up our coats and left the sales office. I was a bit shell-shocked and Keys was still trying to work out the new title that Mr. Fowler had affixed. "Run it by me one more time, will you Marty—what the hell does a *wanker* actually do?"

The next morning I returned to the factory where my admiration of all things American was put to the test. Mr. Fowler praised the increased volume in sales and I was offered a job as a full-on King Arthur Grandfather Clock salesman. I was handed the keys to a gaudy purple Winnebago and decked out in the official uniform, which would have fit a man half again my size. As I stood looking at myself in the mirror, resplendent in my baggy purple attire, I remember thinking that at least I wasn't the first Englishman to be humiliated by Americans. The 1950 World Cup came to mind, as did an unfortunate tea party incident back in 1773.

After three weeks of formal training in the Fairhope factory, I was deemed fit for the road and turned loose on the unsuspecting American public. "Go get 'em Limey!" said George as his secretary shoved another fat cigar into his mouth. "With that accent you can't fail!"

For the next four years, I criss-crossed the US in my garish purple ensemble and sold grandfather clocks in great numbers. I'd occasionally have to duck across the border into Canada to renew my visa, but King Arthur also had a factory in Mississauga, Ontario, so I never missed a step. The border scrutiny was typically unpleasant, and here's how one customs agent summed it up when I questioned the diligence of her search:

"Honey, you're driving a purple motor home with Alabama plates. You've got an English drivers license and a trailer full of grandfather clocks. Bend over and touch your toes."

The King Arthur clocks were quite expensive, so it wasn't long before I had more commission money than I knew what to do with. Eventually, however, my paid tour of America lost its appeal and on Christmas day 1988 I phoned my Mum and Dad and told them that I'd be returning home as soon as my visa expired.

———

These days, whenever an American visits Nursling, I often think of Keys Mitchell, George Fowler and the great number of friendly (and talkative) folks that I met during my brief, yet lucrative career as a nomadic clock peddler in the United States.

I know that many Brits aren't quite as accommodating in their view of Americans, particularly since we've been getting our collective arses handed back to us in a number of sports which *we* invented. That 1-0 beating of England in 1950 still raises my ire, but I'm glad that Americans have taken to fly fishing such as they have, and I always look forward to their visits at Nursling.

They may be a bit too verbose on matters that most Englishmen do not discuss in public, but by God they can fish.

All I Want for Christmas

he rain was beating against the windows, and I could hear the great willow in the garden sweeping across the roof tiles as the fire danced in time with the gusts of wind coming down the chimney.

At first I dismissed the tapping sound as a tree limb bumping against the house. Yet, after a few more moments of staring into the fire, I heard it again, this time with more urgency. Bama also looked up after the second knock, but remained curled at my feet with a curious eye trained my way.

As I turned and looked toward the back door, I wondered what sort of a desperate soul wanders the lanes and knocks in such miserable weather? Probably someone dressed in a great black cloak and clutching some kind of a murder weapon—a huge knife with a jagged blade, no doubt.

I reluctantly shook myself and the dog into life, eased out of the fireside chair, and went to see what kind of a lost soul was out on this godforsaken night. The rain swept into my face as I opened the door and squinted my eyes to see who wanted to be saved. There was no ghastly black cloak; just a dripping man in a brightly coloured oilskin that any self-respecting trawler captain would be proud of. "Alright then, Donny," said the soggy traveller, shedding copious amounts of water into my entryway, "I've got two loaves left over for the chickens; I'll leave them on the side. Even the bloody chub were difficult in this pissing gale!"

Glen Gregory is one of the nicest people that fishes at Nursling and according to those in the know, he's one of the best coarse anglers around. He fishes here after the salmon and trout seasons have closed and it's not unusual to find him out in all weather conditions. He can be a scary-looking chap even when he remembers to put his front teeth in, but he's certainly no murderer.

"Glen, you must be bloody soaked, mate. Come in for a cup of tea?"

I knew he wouldn't accept, but I couldn't stand to see him out there in the cold. In all the years I've known Glen he's never once come into the house. In fact, I think he may be allergic to the indoors.

"No thanks, Donny. I think I'd best get on home and have me tea cheers."

Glen lived about three miles away, and he'd be pulling his homemade trolley laden with fishing gear.

"The water meadows will be flooded mate, put your stuff in the truck and I'll give you a lift home." Again I knew he wouldn't accept. Walking home in the pitch black and the pissing rain was all part of the fishing game for Glen; he always said that it made his tea taste much better.

"Caught the most beautiful dace today, Donny, must have been close on half a pound. Love to see the dace; great to see them in the Test."

Glen had probably been fishing from dawn to dusk. He was soaked to the skin and his voice was trembling with the cold. He had an hour's trek in front of him with nobody waiting for him, no dinner on the table, nobody to talk about the dace with, yet I knew that he was the most contented man in Hampshire. Once home he would dry and clean his fishing gear and write up his diary before even thinking about putting the kettle on.

"Been meaning to ask you, Donny, but you're going to think I'm a right sad bastard. Would it be okay if I fished on Saturday?" He had that look of desperation in his eye; *please say it will be all right Donny.*

"Of course you can fish Saturday, Glen, you can fish any day you want, mate."

"Thanks, Donny, that's brilliant. I think it's a bad forecast again but I'm going to try for some grayling from the Mill Pool, and perhaps a few more of those monster dace!"

With that he pulled down his hat and turned back into the storm to trudge his way home. He stuck his hand up as he closed the gate behind him and I watched as he disappeared down the lane looking like a lifeboat man pulling a golf trolley. The wind was howling and I couldn't hear a thing, but I'd bet money that he was whistling a tune.

When I got back into my chair in front of the fire I looked up at the three red stockings hanging down from the mantle piece, each with a letter to Father Christmas poking out the top. December 25, 2005 was the Saturday to which Glen Gregory referred, and all he wanted for Christmas was to catch a few fish from the Mill Pool, and for me not to think he was a sad bastard.

After the chaos of Christmas morning when all the presents had been opened and mostly forgotten, me and Bama went for a walk along the riverbank, more to escape than to exercise. I'd forgotten about Glen, but there he was on the Mill Pool, huddled under a large brolly to shield himself from the constant drizzle.

A big gleaming smile appeared on his face when I approached, he'd put his teeth in especially for Christmas, and he stuck out his hand and wished me good day.

"Got your two front teeth for Christmas then, Glen?" I asked as we shook hands. He laughed and sat back down on his sun longer and cleared a space so I could sit under the brolly. He rolled himself a smoke and sat back out of the rain with a contented sigh. He had a blanket over his legs and he adjusted the collar on his duffle coat and pulled down a woollen hat over his ears. Another great draw on the cigarette, and again the sigh, as he surveyed all around him.

"I've got me stove and all the makings, Donny, I'll do us a brew in a minute."

I sat there for about fifteen minutes with Glen, had a cup of tea, and politely declined one of his cheese sandwiches. We had a nice visit and when I was about halfway back to the house, something suddenly struck me. I hadn't seen him catch a fish while I'd sat there with him, nor had he even mentioned fishing. This was unheard of, like Manchester United being unable to break down the Accrington Stanley defence. I turned and hurriedly made my way back to the Mill Pool to see whatever was wrong.

Glen was still huddled under his blanket with a fag in one hand and a cup of tea in the other and he greeted me as if he hadn't seen me just minutes earlier, "Alright Donny, want a cuppa, mate?"

His homemade trolley was stood up behind him with his rods still unpacked. "What's up then, Glen, you not fishing today?"

He tapped his cigarette on the side of his chair, let out a sigh, and leaned towards me as he whispered, "Jesus Christ, Donny, it's Christmas day. I thought I'd at least give them the morning off, goodwill and all that."

If Christmas really is all about peace on earth, then Glen Gregory had truly found it.

Fishing or Catching?

n November of 2006 I was lucky enough to secure another invite to fish Scotland's famed River Tweed. Late fall sees the greatest number of salmon in the Tweed, but it's also a time when heavy rains can take the river completely out. In gambling parlance, salmon fishing on a Scottish spate river—even during prime season—is somewhat akin to betting fifty quid on a three-legged donkey at Aintree. There's every chance that you won't even wet a line, let alone actually tighten into something. On this most recent trip, in fact, I had a wonderful time catching absolutely nothing.

This strange tradition involves forking out a small mortgage, looking forward to the fishing all year, the hassle of packing, airports, cancelled flights, lost luggage, and rip-off hotels, only to be told on arrival that it's not stopped raining somewhere on the other side of Scotland, and that has made your beat rise about fifteen feet. At that point, you are obviously expected to accept this as typical of your bad luck and then start saving again for next years' fishing—if, of course, you are lucky enough to be offered it.

The river was actually in good condition during November but none of us caught anything because, according to our happy-go-lucky-laugh-a-minute ghillie, it was slightly too warm, the water was a few inches too low, and we were all wearing the wrong colour underpants.

I caught a plane back to Heathrow from Edinburgh, arriving at 8:30 pm, and hoping to be met by my darling wife. Once we landed I switched my phone back on to let her know I was there. When I got through to her she was still sat in the armchair at home, as there had been a terrible accident and the motorway to the airport had been shut. Yes, I know there are indeed other routes from Southampton to Heathrow, but I've learnt over the years to never question the motives or integrity of a fishing widow.

To cut a painful story short I eventually caught a coach from Heathrow to Southampton via every bloody town, village, and bus stop in southern England and arrived back home at midnight. My wife picked me up from the coach station and on the way home in the car I was telling her all about the horrendous journey: the delays, the filthy coach station full of filthy people, that I was never going to fly from Heathrow again, etc.

"Never mind darling, how many did you catch?" she asked with a total lack of interest.

"Nothing." I replied, "None of us caught a thing but it was absolutely fantastic, we had a great time and my casting was much better than last year."

She looked at me in bewildered silence slowly shaking her head and eventually muttered, "So all that and you never caught a thing? Sorry, I just don't get it."

I totally accept and understand why she doesn't get it; in fact I'd probably be slightly worried if she did. Although I'd lied about the price, she undoubtedly knew that the three days fishing had cost me about a month's wages, I'd had the journey from hell, and caught absolutely cock all, but I'd apparently had a great time. It was a difficult one to comprehend but she just put it down to her general suspicions as a riverkeeper's wife that all salmon fishermen are complete tosspots.

As you may have surmised, I harbour a semi-unhealthy obsession with Atlantic salmon and I never tire of fishing for them. They're a spectacular quarry on rod and line and I'm often amazed at how some that seem totally immersed in the tradition and pageantry of the sport can act so blasé toward such a magnificent fish.

Last summer I was looking after a fisherman at Nursling and pointing out different salmon for him to fish to. He made a pig's ear of casting at most of them but did eventually get it right and a fish took his nymph. He had the fish on for a few seconds but lost it when he allowed his line to fall slack. The fisherman was distraught, but as he reeled in his line, the salmon reappeared in front of us back in its original lay. Once again the fisherman cast his nymph and once again the salmon rose and took. After a ten minute fight the smoothie was ours and we released it back into the river. The fisherman congratulated himself on what he thought a superb piece of fishing, looked at me and said, "What a stupid fish, they're not the brightest of things are they?"

Try as I might, I just could not let that one go.

"No sir, daft as a brush," I told him. "That fish was born in this very river about three years ago and beat nearly insurmountable odds to survive from fry, to parr, to smolt. Weighing only a few ounces, he then negotiated about twenty miles of the Test which is full of rainbows, browns, pike, and avian predators—and finally through the pollution of the estuary and into the sea. From there he swam thousands of miles to his feeding grounds, before the spawning instinct eventually took over. After returning as an adult through miles of ocean laced with drift nets, trawlers, and sea lions, he arrived back at the Test estuary and battled his way through scads of poachers. Now he's back here in the very pool from which he came; a beautiful, bright fifteen-pound salmon that just made the first mistake of his life when he ate *your* fly. Other than that, yes sir, they really are stupid fish. By the way, your baseball cap's on back to front."

We hopelessly addicted salmon anglers may all indeed be tosspots, but you'll never catch us calling a smoothie "stupid."

Falling Tree and Floating Farmer

ama followed the flight path of the three cormorants as they flew across the Drawing Room Pool at the top of the Little River. We both knew where they were headed.

"The bloody Trout Beat, Bama."

He looked up at me with an agreeing nod, *Yep, the bloody Trout Beat, alright. Scraggly, scavenging, thieving bastards. Go get the gun, boss!*

I walked into the house to get the twelve-bore and picked up two cartridges while Bama waited at the back door, knowing the exact routine. We would sneak up to the Trout Beat, the black plague would take off, I'd let fly with both barrels and they'd disappear into the distance laughing. Over time my "gun dog" had outgrown his fear of the shotgun's report, but he remained steadfast in his obvious assessment that his master was a useless tosser when it came to hunting.

When I did on rare occasion actually hit one, he would turn and look toward me with wide-eyed disbelief before setting off at blazing speed to make sure the bastard cormorant was really dead.

As it was we looked upstream and downstream but could

see no sign of the birds, so I sat down on the seat alongside the Lock Hatches Pool with Bama attentively at my side. As we sat there daydreaming and looking at the sluice gates that controlled the levels of the Little River, a massive willow tree on the opposite bank began slowly and very deliberately falling straight towards us. It started with a gentle sway and continued in slow motion before crashing into the pool and showering the dog and me in a tidal wave of water.

There was not a breath of wind, and as I sat there in silence it was only the water dripping from my face that kept me from thinking it was all a surreal dream. I was never really in any danger, the tree had fallen some fifteen feet from where I was sat, but I don't think I would have been able to move even if it had landed on top of me. I was frozen in a dreamy fascination, feeling almost as if I'd witnessed something more evil or unsettling than just a falling tree.

The famous question is always asked about whether or not a falling tree in the middle of a deserted wood makes any noise. Well, I witnessed the crash of a ten-ton willow and I can't remember hearing a thing.

I have seen some incredible sights whilst riverkeeping; things that others who work in the cities will never see. In this case, however, I couldn't help thinking that Mother Nature had made a mistake in her timing and let the tree fall too early. I was supposed to walk up to the pool in the morning and stare in disbelief at the fallen willow thinking, *Must have come down last night. How strange, and not a breath of wind, either.*

Not long after the great willow went down at Lock Hatches, I (indirectly) witnessed another incident whereby something that belongs on dry land ended up in the river.

Geoffrey the farmer, albeit a gentleman farmer with a posh accent, is the archetypal hopeless English fisherman who graces the banks of the chalkstreams not because he wants to, but because his father and grandfather before him did.

He truly is a lovely and unassuming man and one of my favourite visitors. I genuinely look forward to his days at Nursling even though they consist mainly of drinking vast amounts of cheap Scotch and ignoring anything that resembles a fly rod. I reckon Geoffrey the gentleman farmer is in his mid-sixties, even though he looks and moves more like an eighty-year-old stricken with severe arthritis. He prefers the comfort of the fishing lodge to the riverbanks, where he sits for long hours with his nose and cheeks glowing red and a bottle in front of him. He has an infectious laugh and finds just about everything funny, giggling like a naughty boy at anything you say.

Not only does Geoffrey attempt to mind his fishing ancestry, he dresses like them as well. He typically arrives at Nursling wearing fine tweeds and a cravat with a red handkerchief neatly folded in his top pocket. The more pissed he becomes, the louder he giggles and slurs, but his appearance never slips and he's always immaculately dressed—even when sprawled out on the fishing lodge floor.

When he does occasionally venture more than fifty yards from the fishing lodge, it's usually on a mission to find a nice napping spot; and although he always denies it, not taking his rod along is a dead giveaway of an impending snooze in the balsam.

On one of his recent visits he was gone for longer than usual and after a few hours I became concerned and tried to remember just how much Scotch he'd drunk. I found an empty and a half-full bottle in the lodge, which was not an alarming quantity for Geoffrey, but still enough to warrant a quick search.

I was gathering up to leave when he casually wandered into the lodge, put four pieces of his two-piece rod onto the table, and silently poured himself a half pint of Bells. After downing the whiskey he let out a long sigh followed by his trademark giggle. "Been raining cats and dogs, Donny old boy, me jacket's bloody soaked!"

I looked out of the window into the clear blue sky with a burning sun beating down on the parched landscape. "It's about eighty degrees out, Geoffrey, and it hasn't rained in three weeks. My god you're absolutely soaked through—and what happened to your rod?"

By this time Geoffrey was standing in a pool of water looking more confused than usual, but still quietly giggling to himself. "You know Donny, what a damn fool I am, I *thought* I'd taken the wrong rod. Silly of me, who's got mine and we'll swap back? Couldn't cast this one for toffee."

"Well actually that is your rod, Geoffrey. Unfortunately it's got two more bits than it should have, which might explain it being difficult to cast. You're soaking wet and your rod's in pieces, what on earth have you been up to?"

There he stood in the fishing lodge, gently wafting the whiskey under his pickled nose with water drops still rolling down his red face and his hair plastered across his forehead in a style more akin to the Third Reich. He quite obviously had no clue what possible adventure he'd been on for the last four hours, or how he'd ended up with a broken fly rod and sodden underpants.

He put down his empty glass and carefully removed his red handkerchief from the top pocket of his tweed jacket. He took great care in mopping his brow with the dripping wet handkerchief and gasped in disbelief as he wrung it out onto the floor of the fishing lodge. "Christ Donny, I'm sweating like a bloody pig. Definitely coming down with something." With that he sat at the table and poured what remained of the second bottle into his glass.

"You've been in the river haven't you? Either you've fallen in or you fancied a quick dip in the Mill Pool with your clothes on. Whichever way you look at it, Geoffrey, you've definitely been with the fishes."

Soon after Geoffrey trudged off home, I walked down to the Mill Pool where the old farmer had seemingly lost four hours of his life. I followed the path around the pool and carried on downstream past the fish counter and onto the bends near the bottom of the beat. Just before the final bend in the river there is a large ash tree with a seat underneath. The planks were still wet with the imprint, I presumed, of Geoffrey's arse cheeks.

On further inspection I found a great wallow in the bank-side vegetation where it looked as if a drowning cow had attempted to haul itself from the water. From there I slowly made my way back upstream towards the Mill Pool laughing to myself at his escapades and how on earth he'd managed to survive to the age that he had. As I walked past the fish counter, an Environment Agency building which counts all the fish coming into and leaving the river, I thought of the photographs that are automatically taken of all the fish over eighteen inches passing through the counter.

Oh my, Geoffrey, surely not?

I unlocked the door to the counting hut and started to go through the pictures which had been instantly printed out onto a roll of film. Salmon, salmon, probable seatrout, eel, salmon, another seatrout….and….Geoffrey the gentleman farmer. There he was, gliding through the fish counter feet first with his arms folded neatly across his chest and a silly grin on his face. I can only presume that he'd fallen into the Mill Pool and careened downstream through the fish counter before eventually hauling himself out under the ash tree.

I guess we'll never know if he actually recalls his little jaunt downstream. When I showed him the picture two weeks later, he just giggled and shrugged, "Sorry, old boy, for all the fuss, I apologise unreservedly. There's no doubting I've made a bloody fool of myself, again. I mean, for God sakes….a red cravat with a green shirt? Father would be right disappointed!"

The Feminine Touch

s is the case with most salmon anglers on this side of the pond, I am acutely aware of the fact that Miss Georgina Ballantine has, for the better part of a century, held the record for a rod-caught U.K. Atlantic salmon. I have read this a thousand times and have been told it a thousand more. I have seen the pictures, and read enumerable accounts of her sixty-four pounder caught from Scotland's River Tay in the fall of 1922.

She did it. She caught the fish and holds the record—and it's a record that may never be broken. Enough said.

Why is it, then, that Miss Ballantine's name is unfailingly referenced as soon as anyone of the female gender gets to within two miles of a salmon river? Oddly enough, it's not the ladies that usually bring up her name. No, it's more often the male angler. The fishless male, in fact. I've heard the verbal jabs and the attempts to discredit her many a time.

It's all in the pheromones, you know. I've got it on good authority that she's tucking salmon flies down in her knickers. Can't compete with that, now, can we, fellas?

As if on cue, a lady amongst male salmon fishers will invariably cause mention of Miss Ballantine, and on how we pheromone-lacking-blokes can't compete; nothing to do with fishing ability, just an unfair advantage that needs to be pointed out.

Although Miss Ballantine caught her behemoth salmon nearly a hundred years ago, I think that the male attitude towards women fly fishers has finally softened a bit. This is due, in large part, to women standing up against chauvinism in all facets of life and society, not just in fishing.

Whilst playing football many years ago in the Wessex League, a first-ever woman referee was calling a game for my local club, Totton. She was very good, although she produced a red card on one of our defenders after a fairly innocuous looking tackle only minutes into the game.

Afterward I asked my teammate why on earth he had been sent off and what had he said to the ref?

He looked at me with a puzzled expression and replied, "I just told her that she should get back to the bloody ironing board. What's wrong with that?"

He could have called her by any foul name and threatened to break her legs without drawing a foul, but he crossed the line when he trotted out that old number.

There are things that some women may struggle with in competing against men solely because of a physical disadvantage, but fly fishing is not one of them. Indeed, I think that some women have a natural advantage when fly casting, as they must rely on timing and finesse rather than power. The same applies to golfing, where an abuse of power usually equates to similar failings.

I have taught all three of my children to cast a fly rod and they've all become quite good at it. While teaching my two girls when they were aged eight and ten, my son, aged four, casually wandered into the back garden to see what we were doing.

After watching his sisters for a few minutes we asked if he wanted a go. We handed him the rod and he first waved it around like a pirate with a sabre before going through the rudimentary motions of a cast. After a few flailing attempts he managed to get a few yards of line to land straight on the lawn in front of him. At that point his eyes opened wide and a grin spread from ear to ear as he prepared for another effort in front of his sisters. Without even knowing what he was doing, or without being told, he reached down and pulled two or three extra handfuls of line off the reel before his next attempt.

It's obviously an inbuilt man thing; rather like the subconscious scratching of our genitals. We simply cannot help playing with ourselves or casting further than is needed, especially in front of the ladies.

Female fly fishers are usually much easier to teach, and I'm convinced that this comes from their willingness to listen and learn new things through small steps. The male ego far too often takes over before the basic elements of casting have been learned.

In Scotland I have watched with fascination as ladies meticulously cover every inch of water from their toes to mid-river. The man, on the other hand, immediately attempts to cast as far across river as possible while deliberately ignoring the easy, girly bit right in front of him. His main goal is in attempting to hit the man on the opposite bank, who of course is doing exactly the same thing from the other side. This testosterone casting duel is an important, almost vital, part of the male salmon fishing experience and only adds to the chances of another fishless day.

A percentage of the population—men and women—will simply never become accomplished salmon anglers no matter which hormones or pheromones are involved. It's a punishing grind that's not for the delicately wired, but after my most recent trip to the Tweed in 2008, I now have newfound respect for those ladies that do put in the time to become great salmon anglers.

For the past several years, my mates and I have fished the Lower Mertoun beat of the Tweed. It's a veritable salmon fishing paradise and each year we stay in a beautiful bed and breakfast owned by Ally and Charles Bremner in the nearby town of Melrose. They're wonderful hosts who always take care of the little things that matter to travelling anglers, like an extra flask of soup when it's cold and copious amounts of liquor when we return fishless. Ally is always interested to hear of our day's fishing and we feel obliged to tell her of our captures, near misses, and hard luck salmon tales. Before this most recent trip, however, I never elaborated too much, thinking that she wouldn't really understand and was only asking out of politeness.

On the third morning of our trip, Ally casually mentioned that she was going fishing herself. She modestly announced that there was very little chance of her catching anything and she would probably just use the time to practise her Spey casting, which was a "bit rusty." Having never seen her cast, I gave her a few useful tips and suggested one or two very basic things for her to try.

The next day, our last on the Tweed, we asked Ally if she would like to come down and see the Mertoun Beat; if it was okay with the ghillie, perhaps she could also have a cast or two. Sure enough, Ally turned up early afternoon with her waders on and the usual flask of soup and box of sandwiches. As we all sat in the hut and talked of fishing and salmon, she was on the edge of her seat and appeared mesmerised by the Lower Mertoun beat and the prospect of fishing it.

I suggested that she fish through the pool outside the hut with the ghillie while the other rod, Graham, fished further upstream. I sat there for a few minutes while Ally tackled up, but then decided to join Graham upriver so that she might not feel nervous in front of spectators.

After an hour or so, Graham and I slowly made our way back to the hut and talked of perhaps spending a little time with Ally, encouraging her and sympathising that this Spey casting game is not as easy as it looks.

When we got to within a few yards of the hut, we saw Ally fishing midstream and the ghillie sat inside and drinking a cup of tea. We were surprised that he had abandoned the fair lady to the river, and we almost fought each other past the hut to save this poor damsel in distress. It was just as I was about to call out to her that we were coming to her rescue that she lifted her rod to make another cast.

With finesse and timing that I had only seen among a few expert Spey casters, Ally ripped the line from the water with one sharp lift and snapped into an impossibly perfect snake roll that curled past her head into a single Spey. Forming an immaculate "D" behind her, she then punched it thirty-five yards toward the opposite bank in arrow straight fashion. She looked behind her and smiled at us as the line landed and the fly turned over quite perfectly. Then she glanced back at the line, rolled a perfect upstream mend, and remarked, "This downstream wind makes it difficult from the true left, doesn't it?" Not quite satisfied with that attempt, she then put her left hand on top and made a double Spey cast off her left shoulder resulting in the line once again shooting across the river in an unnerving straight line.

I looked at Graham who was stood next to me with his mouth agape. He then turned to me and whispered, "Bloody hell. Looks like poached eggs is not all she's good at."

I nodded in agreement.

"You go and help her, Donny. She can cast that line further than I can hit a five iron."

We both snuck back to the hut and sat down next to the ghillie and tried not to let her see us watching out the window.

For the rest of that afternoon, there was not one mention of Miss Ballantine.

If ever you're looking to stay in Melrose, try Ally and Charles Bremner at Buccleuch House. You'll not find a better B&B in the Scottish Borders. Excellent lodgings, superb food, lashings of drink, charming company—and if you're really lucky, you might get to see the landlady cast.

Heaven, Hell, or Chicago?

spend most of my days thinking about how we can help the salmon, but I fully appreciate that in this day and age most people have far more important things to think about than the decline of a certain species of fish. I think about such trivial things because I have in a way decided to opt-out of the mainstream way of life. I still have my fair share of real world hassle, but compared to many, I have an easy way of living away from the hustle and bustle of twenty-first century life.

Although I live only a few miles from Southampton, I do at times feel detached from the reality of the times in which we live. I feel old-fashioned and that I was perhaps born fifty years too late. Maybe my school report was right. Maybe I am just too nice, or perhaps too naïve to survive in these times.

I became a riverkeeper to avoid such pressure but I'm finding it more and more difficult to repel the intrusion of modern living. I have a little box of instant communication with me at all times which I find annoyingly useful, yet it prevents me from fully escaping, no matter how much solitude I seek.

Everything nowadays has to be immediate—communication, news, food, credit, shopping, everything. In my simpleton's view, this world of instant gratification in which we now live has only added to people's stress and frustration levels.

Recently, I went into a local bank to buy some Euros and after taking some details the smiling cashier asked for my account number.

"I'm afraid I haven't got a bank account here."

The cashier, still smiling, asked me whom I banked with.

"Nobody, I haven't got a bank account anywhere."

The smile was replaced with a vacant stare, and he then went on, "Well I'm afraid that makes things a little difficult because we don't accept credit cards on these transactions."

"Actually it doesn't make it more difficult because I haven't got a credit card either."

The cashier was visibly startled, and although he didn't call me a backward country hick that is undoubtedly what he was thinking. He said he would be just a moment and then walked slowly around the desks behind him talking quietly to his colleagues. As he moved from desk to desk the occupants were left staring in my general direction at the bum with no cheques or credit cards.

After completing the circuit the cashier returned to me with a bemused expression. "So let me get this right," he smirked, "you've got no bank account or cheque book and you've got no credit card?" A self-satisfied grin crept back onto his face as he thought of his next smarmy reply.

"That's right."

"Could you then perhaps enlighten me on exactly how you planned on paying for these Euros?"

Matching his condescending tone, I fired right back, "Yes I'll enlighten you. MONEY is what I'm going to pay with. Cash, wonga, pound notes, spondullies; you know the stuff."

I took out my cash and laid it on the counter. He just stood staring at the curled up fifty-pound notes like a cat mesmerised with a nearly-dead mouse. Without breaking stare, he slowly said, "I'm sorry sir but we don't accept cash."

There was an embarrassing silence, so I stood staring at him for a few extra moments, just to prolong his discomfort.

"So you're a bank, but you don't accept cash?"

"That's right sir," he said, head still bowed, "I'm afraid we don't for Euros."

The lobby was awkwardly quiet and a number of the employees and patrons stared my way. Had I farted out loud, I doubt the result would have been any less dramatic.

I picked up my money and walked towards the door where I met a lady coming in from the sidewalk. When I stepped aside and held the door open for her, she looked at me with an annoyed expression and said, "Actually I'm quite able to open the door myself, thank you very much."

As I drove back to the river and my own little out-of-date world, I thought again of my school report. Has it really gotten to the point that politeness is regarded as condescending behaviour? When my friends and family find me enthusiastically immersed in the meticulous details of bridge building, weed cutting, or fly casting, they often tease and suggest that maybe I need to get out more.

Maybe I don't, maybe I'm better off where I am.

I was always taught that it was polite to open a door or give up my seat for a lady, and I plan to teach my son the same manners. The fact that this particular lady seemed annoyed doesn't make it wrong, but politeness does sadly appear to be a dying fashion.

I have noticed over time that it's only the elderly, these days, that say, "good morning" to each other. If I were to extend that courtesy to some of the younger set that live near me, they would either assume that I was a complete nutter, or tell me to mind my own damn business.

I can't understand why people have to be so hard-nosed and aggressive, and I'm sure that the breakdown in simple manners has lead to the alarming increase in anti-social behaviour that we're now seeing.

Today there seems to be an abrupt precipice between right and wrong. The grey areas of ethics and accountability seem to be eroding, and many now live their lives balanced precariously on the edge with little concern that there's no safety net at the foot of the cliff.

In 1984 I was hitchhiking on the outskirts of New York when a pleasant couple offered me a ride. It turned out they were on their way to church and they had seen me as an opportunity to score some religious brownie points; pick up the waif and the Lord will love us.

Not yet knowing my role in this arrangement, I sat back in my seat wondering what we were going to have for dinner and whether or not the nice lady would wash my clothes for me. Little did I know that I was nothing more than a pawn for them to parade in front of their congregation as a saved soul picked mercifully from of the gutter.

It was a big church with at least a couple of hundred followers and after being introduced to the pastor I was asked to sit at the front looking out towards the congregation. Apparently I was to be a living, breathing example of what could happen if you wander from the straight and narrow.

The service seemed to go on for a long time and I would have dozed off were it not for the fixed gaze of a couple of hundred pairs of eyes. When the pastor abruptly shouted my name, I sat bolt upright as he began to lambast my lifestyle and tell the wide-eyed parishioners precisely where I'd gone wrong in life.

"This young man from across the water in England has come to our country like a lost soul, wandering the land not knowing which way to turn," the pastor preached. "Should he go east, west, north or south? It is a big decision that will affect the rest of his life, and we need to pray for young Marty Donovan, this lost Englishman, and hope that the Lord guides him down the right path. Stand up young man and raise your hands to the Lord!"

I slowly eased my heathen body out of the chair and lifted my arms up as if surrendering to an unseen enemy. I winced with alarm as the pastor suddenly proclaimed in a booming voice, "Hallelujah and praise the LORD! In which direction are you going Marty Donovan—are you going to HEAVEN, or are you going to HELL?"

In a hushed, trembling voice, fully expecting to be struck down by a bolt of lightning, I cleared my throat and nervously mumbled my reply, "Err…uh, neither…I'm actually going to Chicago."

That nice lady cooked me a lovely dinner, but she never did wash my clothes.